The Romance of Reason

An Adventure in the Thought of Thomas Aquinas

by Montague Brown

Saint Bede's Publications
Petersham, Massachusetts

Saint Bede's Publications
P.O. Box 545, Petersham, Massachusetts 01366-0545

Printed in the United States of America

99 98 97 96 95 94 93   5 4 3 2 1

Library of Congress Cataloging-in-Publication Data
Brown, Montague, 1952-
   The romance of reason : an adventure in the thought of
Thomas Aquinas / by Montague Brown.
            p.   cm.
   Includes bibliographical references.
   ISBN 0-932506-96-8
   1. Thomas, Aquinas, Saint, 1225?-1274.   I. Title.
B765. T54B7335 1993   93-20290
189' .4--dc20   CIP

Contents

To my mother and father
first lights of Love and Wisdom

Preface

I have entitled this book *The Romance of Reason* because it seems to me that, contrary to much popular belief, reason plays a rather dashing and heroic role in the story of our lives. Thus, I am using the word romance in the medieval sense of a tale of chivalry. Reason is the hero who breaks the chains of our prejudice, saving us from the prison of our comfortable acquiescence in the way of the world, to lead us on adventures full of excitement and wonder. The book happens to be about Thomas Aquinas because it was through a trial by combat with his thought that I found my own comfortable ideas about what is true and good defeated and myself caught up in this great adventure of reason.

This book is not meant to be a comprehensive study of the thought of Thomas Aquinas. Its brevity alone makes that obvious. It does not even attempt to give a general survey of the scope of his work. Rather, it focuses on a few great ideas and the way in which Aquinas came to them. It is a study of reason, not as the last word in the conversation that is life, but as the invitation to explore and discover a new life of meaning. The book is an attempt to put some very exciting and surprising thinking in non-technical language so as to make it accessible to the interested reader who may not have the time or fortitude to tackle the difficult philosophical terms and immense volume of Aquinas's work. The book remains, however, a book about thinking. The ideas are hard, not because they are esoteric or overly complex, but because they are so very simple and fundamental. To focus on their simplicity takes some effort. My hope is that this presentation of the thought of Aquinas may lead the reader into a world of thinking that opens new vistas of joy and wonder.

I make no claims for the originality of the work. In the first place, I am interpreting the thought of Aquinas. In the second place I have been aided in the interpretation by some who understand Aquinas far better than I. Three sources of inspiration I need acknowledge at the outset. To Herbert McCabe I owe much in terms of understanding Aquinas's notion of creation and how this notion affects our understanding of the relationship between God and human beings. The work of Bernard Lonergan has helped clarify for me Aquinas's theory of knowledge. And from the tradition of natural law ethics developed out of Aquinas by Germain Grisez, John Finnis, and Joseph Boyle I have learned much about the basics of ethics. However, as I said before, this is a book about thinking, and in the process of thinking I may not have interpreted either Aquinas or his commentators as they in all cases might have wished. For this I apologize in advance. However, such forays and excursions after truth may be allowed to be in the spirit of Aquinas himself who said that philosophy is not to say what other people have said, but what the truth of the matter is. I hope that my excursions have not wandered too far from the truth, and I invite the reader into that adventure, unique to every knower, of making the truth one's own.

I am indebted to Dr. Johann Moser for reading an earlier draft of this work and making many valuable suggestions as to clarity, structure, and style.

I
Reason and Wonder

It is often thought that reason and wonder are opposites, even enemies. Whether this is, in fact, true or not, it is easy enough to see how such an notion could arise. To reason one's way to knowledge is to tame the wonderful. To wonder is to live beyond the pale of rational certainty.

Since we only wonder about what we do not understand, if reason helps us understand, then apparently it works to destroy wonder. We wonder about many different kinds of things. There is wonder in beauty. There is wonder in creative imagination. There is wonder in friendship and love. There is wonder in religious faith. Each of these kinds of wonder may seem to be threatened by reason. Rational scrutiny may indeed dispel the admiration of beauty; logical rigor may stifle creativity; intense analysis of friendship may very well end it; and understanding may destroy or at least displace faith. If we cherish these wonders, and they appear well worth cherishing, then perhaps we had better man the walls against the forces of reason.

Just as reason appears to be antagonistic to wonder, wonder, for its part, looks like the arch-enemy of reason. Reason provides us with certain and objective information about our world. Wonder considers that which can never be completely comprehended and systematized–that which is, to some degree, out of this world. Devotees of reason often consider the things with which wonder is concerned to be unreal, and wonder to be mere infatuation, illusion, or superstition. To be enlightened is to be free from all irrational tendencies, to stand firm in the light of demonstrated truth. If we honor truth and honesty, and these certainly do appear worthy of our esteem, then perhaps we had better close our ears to the siren songs of wonder.

Thus, the battle lines are drawn. Romantics fear reason, for it threatens what they treasure–the spirit of adventure and love. Rationalists ignore wonder (perhaps also out of fear), for wonder threatens what they treasure–the coherence of the system of explanation which they have so painstakingly put together.

Over against both these views stands the view of Thomas Aquinas. Reason and wonder are not enemies but closest of companions. Far from seeking to destroy wonder, reason is its greatest champion. And far from misleading reason, wonder is reason's very life. It is my contention that, in his inclusive embrace of both reason and wonder, Aquinas is truer to the nature of reason than the rationalist, and truer to the nature of wonder than the romantic. Pledging himself to the true and the good, Thomas Aquinas finds that reason and wonder are not irreconcilable foes, but allies in the fight to liberate and protect the human heart.

At the center of the life of reason, there is the wonder that awakens one to the call to truth. Before any rational formulations or definitions are made, one has a question. Something awakens us to awareness of a world and a self and to a desire to understand each. This desire to know is wonder. If we never wondered about things, we would never try to understand them and hence would never, obviously, succeed in understanding them. In this way wonder gives birth to the life of the mind.

Not only is wonder the origin of reason, it is also the sustainer of reason. Without wonder (that is, without questions) reason stagnates. By nature reason is a dynamic quest. When separated from wonder, it sinks into static cycles of repeated formulas. Such formulas, once mastered, are easy and comfortable, but without life. For reason to become settled into a state in which some fixed pattern of statements is accepted as perfectly conveying the truth about reality is for reason to die the death of triviality. Life is not reducible to such rigid systematization. Advances in knowledge of any kind only come about because people have further questions, because people wonder about the way things are. Of course, the careful ordering and working out of a problem (taking a systematic approach to something) is a necessary and vital part of learning, but it is only a part. Any systematization is always an abstraction from reality, never quite touching the living center of what is real. To rest in a system is to rest from reason, and to rest from reason is to rest from a fully human life. Shakespeare's works are unthinkable without wonder; they were certainly not deductions from previous literature. Nor did relativity theory evolve necessarily from Newtonian mechanics. Without wonder, there would be no creativity for the scientist as well as the artist. Reason's continuing achievements depend on wonder.

Yet wonder does not triumph over reason, for we cannot take wonder without reason, as the romantic would counsel. Not only would such a move be wrong, but we actually cannot do it. We only wonder because we are beings who can reason, who can distinguish and clarify and arrive at truth. Wonder is not the end of being human but an ever-new beginning. To have a question is to want to know an answer. It is only because we are the kind of creatures who can reason to the truth that we have questions and that we wonder. The fulfillment of plants and animals is not to know the truth, and so they do not wonder. Thus, a life of wonder cannot be the unreflective, spontaneous life which the pure romantic (nineteenth-century variety) seeks to embrace by imitating the rhythms of instinctual and unselfconscious nature. Wonder is the potential for knowing: it is the desire to know. Insofar as it is actualized, it is responding to a call to truth. Thus, it is natural for wonder to issue in propositions which try to express precise meaning and certainty. That there is indeed something to know is the only possible explanation for there being a desire to know, for our being children of wonder.

But if understanding is the fulfillment of wonder, does not this mean that reason is, after all, triumphant, that wonder is but a temporary illusion of mystery which will in the end be clarified and hence destroyed? Aquinas's answer to this question is "Try it and see." Follow reason with full devotion. After all, there can be no reason not to: our very wonder tells us to. And this is what Aquinas does. He has a deep confidence in reason's ability to get to the truth. The truth, however, turns out to be rather more mysterious than the modern ideal of scientific systematization might suggest. Reason, given full rein, enters into a symbiotic relationship with wonder: meaning leads to mystery, and mystery feeds meaning. On the one hand, what we can learn about reality leads us deeper and deeper into wonder at reality. The known draws the knower face-to-face with the unknown: meaning reveals mystery. On the other hand, the wonder at what we do not completely understand leads us deeper and deeper into understanding. What is unknown calls the knower forth to know: mystery is not unmeaning but deeper meaning.

Let us sketch out in some more detail the way Aquinas takes in seeking out the truth. Some philosophers, most notably Plato, held that all our ideas are innate. We are born with full knowledge of all things, and what we call learning is merely a process of remembering what we already know. Following Aristotle, Aquinas says that this position is simply contrary to common sense. One is conscious of coming to know, of learning through experience. But Plato was not completely wrong. We are born with two aspects of knowing that are innate, for the ability and the desire to know are not themselves learned, but rather are presupposed to any learning. However, the specific content of what is known is not innate. We draw the content from our experience of the world in which we live.

Besides accounting for our experience of coming to know, this position of Aristotle and Aquinas also explains why we are unities of mind and body: our very operation of thinking requires sensation to supply it with its initial data upon which to work. In Plato, the body is the explanation for our forgetting what we really know. The human being is really the soul, which knows innately all that is true. The body makes us forget the truth. And so, there is no explanation for us being embodied. In fact, the body is the enemy of reason. Contrary to this position, Aristotle and Aquinas insist that the body is part of the explanation for our knowing, and indeed part of the definition of what it is to be human. The mind draws its understanding, in the first instance, out of what is sensed. The body provides the mind with data for thinking. It is the material things of everyday experience which are the first immediate objects of knowledge.

Now, when we come to try to understand these things of our experience, success is not instantaneously complete. We run up against a continual barrage of existing things which do not fit our definitions and systems of order. From these meetings questions arise, and we find ourselves in a process of deepening understanding. The first attempts to formulate the meaning of reality are improved by later reformulations. Why do we make these reformulations? We do so either because we recognize that something was imperfect in our prior understanding or because there is something new to be assimilated. A new question arises which unsettles our confidence in the completeness of our understanding, and so we attempt to understand better. The child's growth in awareness is a case in point. The blur becomes pattern of light and shade, becomes source of food, becomes protector, becomes loving mother, becomes independent human being to be loved as well as to love me. The mother, of course has not gone through all these reformulations of reality; it is the child's understanding of her mother which has changed. And the child's understanding changes because new dimensions of reality penetrate consciousness. The same is true of other knowing processes. One learns the right way to get to the Children's Museum in Boston through reality (in the form of one-way streets going in circles) continually breaking in on what one thought was the truth about how Boston is laid out. In physics, Aristotle is reformulated in Newton, and Newton in Einstein, because reality upsets the formulations which scientists have made. Knowing is a quest led by questioning which arises in response to a world.

This does not mean that we have no certain knowledge along the way. We know for sure that $2+2=4$, that Australia is surrounded by water, that a bedpost is not a hedgehog. It is just that, as reality is never comprehended by any one adequate definition, there is always more to know. Being sensitive to what we do not know is an essential ingredient for the life of the mind. Under the influence of wonder, our knowledge becomes more comprehensive, deeper and more meaningful. It is not that all knowledge we now possess must eventually be abandoned in the progress of reason. As a matter of fact, this is one of the things upon which Aquinas most stridently insists: never give up truth in the face of other truth. Short of absolute contradiction, one must never cast away one truth in the name of another truth, however strange bedfellows the two truths may appear to be. To do so is to fundamentally renounce our rationality. It was Aquinas's discovery that reason, if followed devotedly, yields truth far more wonderful than anyone could have expected. Reason provides us with access to a world much more mysterious than we had thought. As I said before, for something to be mysterious is not for it to be inaccessible or unapproachable because of a fundamental lack of meaning or incoherence, but rather for it to be recognized as clearly more meaningful than we can fully grasp. Mystery is deeper meaning, not unmeaning.

When Thomas Aquinas applied himself to the great philosophical (human) questions, such as "What is the nature of reality?" or "What is it to be a human being?" or "How does the ultimate source of reality interact with human nature?" he found himself with irreducibly multiple truths. For example, he found that reason's attempts to explain the universe completely yield, on the one hand, knowledge of comprehensive natural causes of the order and operations of the universe and, on the other, knowledge that there is a cause of the very existence of the universe. No explanations about how the universe conforms to basic physical laws can explain why there is a universe in the first place; and the understanding that there is a creator of the universe tells us nothing about the way the universe itself operates. Aquinas also found that reason's attempts to explain the nature of the human being uncover the oddity that we are at once material and immaterial. When we examine what it is to be human, we find ourselves to be both sensing and thinking beings. This implies that we are material and immaterial, for one cannot sense without a body, and what is purely material cannot think. A computer, for example, while it may be said to have information, does not know that it has information. For this reason, the computer cannot reevaluate the information it has and formulate a new structure of meaning, nor can it recognize or handle ambiguity, which is essential to communication and growth in understanding. We want to know exactly how these irreducibly multiple truths fit together, but our actual understanding falls short of reconciling all meanings. We seek a perfectly unified explanation, but find truths in tension.

Faced with such a problem, what is one to do? The quickest and most obvious way of reaching unity is to deny one truth or the other. Thus, on the question of the relation between God and science, some claim that there cannot be a God because God could not be verified by scientific method. Others claim that, since there is a God, science is not really legitimate knowledge, having been superseded by God's Revelation. Or, considering the puzzle of human nature, some claim that we are purely material, that thinking is a merely mechanical process; others claim that we are purely immaterial with sensing and all material reality deriving somehow from thought–"It's all in the mind."

In this quickest way of handling truths in tension, one truth is virtually ignored. The attempt is made to handle the evidence covered by the truth ignored in terms of the truth chosen. When this happens, an obvious and commonsensical explanation is replaced by one obscure and esoteric. It is absurd for science to adopt the unproven axiom that God does not exist (implied in the scientific method, which holds that all that is real is material) and then assume that it has proved that God does not exist. It is equally absurd for the romantic fundamentalist to assume that because God created the universe, there really is no universe (the object of scientific explanations) but only God. As to the issue of human nature, it is ridiculous to explain a stubbed toe in terms of immaterial causes alone, or to explain something that transcends time and place (thought) in terms merely of time and place. The efforts of these reductionists to explain the truth that is in tension with their first axiom (science or God, mind or matter) lead to ridiculous conclusions. Thus, the problem with this quickest and most obvious way of dealing with two truths in tension is that it succeeds in achieving unity only at the expense of truth. One truth learned by reason is abandoned in favor of another. In short, this way provides an explanation by denying reason. Reason is sacrificed to reason, and we end in absurdity.

The question must always be: what is the evidence which shows that a claim to truth is legitimate or illicit? Unless there is good evidence that science rules out the existence of God, or that God rules out the possibility of science, one is not in a position to deny one or the other. Unless there is good evidence that our materiality rules out our immateriality or vice versa, one is in no position to deny one or the other. The inability to formulate perfectly how two truths are one in reality is no grounds for denying either truth. Only obvious contradiction, based on evidence, can justify rejection.

Rationalism, with its fundamental insistence that all reality be explained in terms of a closed system, turns out to falter on irrationality.[1] Rationalism turns out to be not the triumph of reason but its failure, and it takes reason to show this. Reason discovers evidence for the mysterious nature of reality. In order to dispel the mystery, rationalism rejects what reason has shown to be true. Oddly enough, this fault of rationalism may well issue from a lapse in reason itself, from reason falling under the sway of imagination. No one can imagine how the apparently antagonistic explanations of reality can be true simultaneously. No one can imagine how God and the laws of physics can operate simultaneously, or how the human being can be simultaneously material and immaterial. It is impossible to imagine such a thing, for images depend on sense experiences (immediate or remembered) which are of the physical world; and since no two physical things can be simultaneously in the same place at the same time, no two images can be held simultaneously by the same person about the same aspect of the same thing.

But thinking is not the same as imagining. We can understand how two activities may go on simultaneously, for this is the very basis of understanding anything at all, and

---

[1]By "closed system" I mean something like Euclidean geometry, in which all conclusions follow obviously and necessarily from self-evident axioms.

we can understand how one activity may operate simultaneously in two places, for all communication requires this. You sense and understand simultaneously that the black letters are different from the white page: you see this (there is a material activity going on), and you know this (there is an immaterial activity going on). If I speak to a friend and he understands me, then my understanding and his understanding are the same. They must be or there would be no communication. Hence, although we cannot imagine it, we can know that two activities may operate simultaneously and that one activity may operate simultaneously in two places. We must not let imagination dominate our thinking. To do so is to cease to think. The rationalist, with his insistence on a deductively ordered system to explain reality, is not thinking so much as picture-thinking. He is seeing reality as a map of exclusive alternatives, with every alternative reducible at last to a perfectly clear first axiom.

A simple way to explain the danger of rationalism is to say that, although we all naturally want to know the truth, there are two rather divergent ways of approaching the fulfillment of our desire. We may patiently and humbly respond to the evidence we receive, ever open to new data and dimensions of meaning. Or we may take the short cut (the more usual path, I am afraid) and declare my truth to be the truth. This is the pitfall of the system builder. Reality is forced to conform to a conception, rather than our conceptions responding to reality. This attempt to force reality into the limits of what one knows is the destruction of reason. One must not neglect the fundamental component of knowing which is the judging whether one's insight is correct. The question arises: "Am I right to think that this concept is true to the nature of reality?" The act of ignoring this vital component of knowing can lead one to shut off, arbitrarily, any further questions and to assume that one's concept comprehends reality. Thus, one makes one's unexamined assumption (perhaps that all is mind, or all is matter) the center of one's system for understanding the world, and then co-ordinates all elements of reality to fit in a deductive scheme under the first uncritical assumption. What does not fit the scheme is rejected as unreal. This is the undo-ing of reason.

To avoid this disaster, one must have a moral commit-ment to finding the truth, to hearing the questions, and to being open to the evidence. This is the love component without which philosophy (literally "the love of wisdom") must die the death of triviality. It does not matter whether one has achieved a closed system if the system does not respond to reality. In fact, no system can com-prehend reality, for the meaning of reality lies ultimately in the mystery of deepening meaning. This is what Aqui-nas understood and what this book is all about.

A commitment to real thinking discovers these mysteries of God and human beings to be true to reality, not with a knowledge that puts to death all wonder, but with a knowledge that recognizes the truth of its vision, but also its limitations. For our thinking is a reaching for reality, not its rule. It is reason which tells us rationalism is dead and untrue. What is needed to reconcile truths in tension is a higher viewpoint which can allow for what is true on both sides. A case where such a higher viewpoint has not been reached we call a mystery. A mystery is not a con-tradiction, although it may appear to be so. Mystery is not the destroyer of reason's life, but its spur. The presence of mystery is the invasion of a question, of a wonder which awakens reason to life. This is the normal way scientific knowledge progresses, as, in response to the unexpected, it moves to explanations of reality which are more and more comprehensive. But when one reaches the ultimate questions of reality, to which the answers are these truths in tension, then the higher viewpoint which shows precisely how the truths fit together escapes our grasp. At the frontier of reason, we have a reach into mystery for meaning.

Four of these mysterious double-edged truths I have chosen to examine in this book. In formulating them, Aquinas goes beyond the wisdom of the great Greek philosophers and establishes himself as perhaps the greatest philosopher of all times.[2] Each pair of truths in tension is a puzzle eliciting wonder, encouraging thought and deeper understanding which, in turn, elicit deeper wonder.

The first pair of truths in tension concerns the relationship between science and God. If the natural explanations of science reveal the universe to be run by its own necessary laws, why is there a need for another explanation in terms of a creating God? Or, looked at from the other side, if all depends on God completely, what happens to the independent explanations of science?

The second pair concerns the nature of the human being. If the human being is a material being, which seems obvious, how do we explain the fact that people can know things that transcend the material conditions of time and space? Or, if we take full cognizance of the implications of

---

[2]Aquinas himself would never have said this. He is forever putting his insights into the mouths of his predecessors. And although I am concerned in this book to show the advances Aquinas made on Plato and Aristotle, he owes so much to each that I must not leave the impression that his thinking is without deep roots in the great Greek philosophers.

thought, how do we explain how an immaterial faculty can be joined to a material thing?

The third and fourth pairs of truths in tension arise out of the interrelations of God and human beings. The third concerns the relationship between free choice and providence. If everything is completely dependent on God, and hence all things must happen according to his will, how am I free to choose? Or, if my choices are free, how can God rule them? The fourth concerns the place of God and human nature in morality. If God is the source of morality by being the cause of all things, is morality a matter of religious acceptance of what God has revealed? Or, if morality is a matter of what natural reason can make out, is God unimportant or superfluous to what we do?

The romantic might look at these tensions between truths and say: "See, this just goes to show the impotence of reason; reason cannot help us discover what is true and good." From the other side, the rationalist might look on these tensions and simply declare the problems to be false, ignoring the independence of one of the truths in tension and attempting to explain it away according to the accepted principles of his system. Thomas Aquinas steers a straight course between the romantic and the rationalist and refuses to reject reason (with the romantic) or any of the mysterious fruits of reason (with the rationalist). What he finds by doing so is that the apparent paradoxical positions turn out to be, not the self-destruction of reason or the results of bad logic, but the mutually supporting pillars of a truth that is living and dynamic. This is Aquinas's method: keep all truth. Never exclude from consideration what has meaningful evidence. This method reveals reality as more mysterious than we had thought. Since mystery is not the enemy of meaning but its source and protector, the discovery that reason lives on the edge of wonder should not be cause for alarm, but for affirmation and celebration of the surprise that is the world and our life. Reason shows itself to be alive in wonder.

The wonder in beauty, the wonder in friendship, and the wonder in faith–all these are not threatened or destroyed by reason. Reason turns out to be protector and defender of wonder, born of it, nourished by it, and loyal to it. Far from being the deathly specter who reduces the robust excitement of life to a skeleton of irrelevance, reason is the great romantic hero who frees us to live in love and wonder. Thinking does not chain life to a system, but unlocks doors to vistas of life and creativity which we could never imagine. If we are careful to think, and not to let our senses, imagination, and emotions drag us around, then we shall find that what the world is, what we are, and what we are doing here become not less interesting and appealing, but, on the contrary, grow ever richer in significance and wonder.

The alternative visions of the world and ourselves which reason uncovers may indeed, at first, appear as irreconcilable antagonists which threaten to destroy each other and our confidence in the world and ourselves. But if we will only put appearances aside and think about what is real, we shall find the antagonism turned allegiance and our confidence restored and deepened. It is only when we reach beyond the senses, beyond the imagination, and beyond the emotions to thought that we recognize reason, not as the one who threatens our cherished beliefs and loves, but as the great champion of all that is human.

And so the story of reason is not the history of the gradual and inevitable displacement of the wonderful and mysterious. It is the story of the child's wonder lost so that the adult might wonder more deeply and with greater certainty. It is the story of the quest for true freedom and love. It is the story of the slaying of human dragons and of false gods. It is a story of losing home, only to find a new home in which all that was good and true in the old is retained and transformed, and the only loss–that of fear and ignorance–is gain. It is the romance of reason.

II
The Creating God and the
Universe of Science

The notions of a creating God and of a comprehensive natural science have been around since God gave Revelation to the Hebrews and the ancient Greeks embarked on systematic philosophy. The relationship between these two notions has been marked by a kind of tension, if not antagonism. If science gives truth, it would seem that there is no creating God; for science is about the necessary laws of the universe, and if the laws are necessary, they would not appear to depend on prior cause. If, on the other hand, God is the cause of everything that exists, then it would seem true to say that what God says goes, and that the "necessary" laws of science are in fact just arbitrary whims of the divine will which could be changed at any moment. To resolve this tension, science tends to relegate the notion of a creating God to the realm of religion, banishing it from natural reason. On the other side, many religious people look upon scientific explanation and research as a threat to faith, regarding natural reason as a stumbling stone, something to be rejected if one would be saved.

Actually, this scenario is not really quite true historically, for these traditions developed in isolation from each other, and so the tension between them was not immediately apparent to either. The Bible says that all that God created is very good, and that man is to rule over creation. Now to rule requires knowledge of what is to be ruled, and so there would seem to be nothing in the Biblical tradition adverse in principle to science. As for the Greeks, they never directly rejected the notion of creation, for they did not consider creation from nothing to be a possibility. They did, however, share the common dictum "from nothing, nothing comes," and so, if faced with the radical statement that the world is created from nothing, they would probably have rejected it in the name of this principle. But, as I said, the ancient Greeks never really considered the possibility of creation. For them, it was apparent that the world had always been around; they were concerned with explaining its order and structure–that is, with giving a scientific interpretation of a world whose existence was taken for granted.

When, however, these two traditions met in full force with the mingling of Christian and Greek cultures in the early centuries after Christ, the inherent tensions became apparent. At the time, there were three philosophical schools of thought that were prevalent in the Hellenistic world: Stoicism, Epicureanism, and Neoplatonism. Epicureanism and Stoicism were forms of materialism which held, as the name suggests, that all that is real is made of matter. To these schools of thought, the notion of an immaterial being making all of the material world out of nothing made no sense whatsoever. Neoplatonism, on the other hand, recognized immaterial beings as the highest of things, and saw the material world as almost unreal. For this reason, it appears that Neoplatonism might be quite compatible with creationism. However, this proves to be untrue. Although Neoplatonism did teach that all things came forth from one first immaterial principle, the manner of the coming forth was diametrically opposed to the Biblical tradition. In the latter, God is said to create the world freely out of nothing, and when he has created he observes that it is all very good. In Neoplatonism, however, the coming forth of all things from "The One" happens of necessity, and the last stage of this emanation–the material world–is regarded as hardly real and in some way fundamentally evil.

For Neoplatonism the philosopher's quest should be a turning away from the material world, which is bad, in order to join oneself more closely to the good, immaterial principle of that world. This philosophy, of course, had trouble figuring out how what is evil could emanate from what is good, but the Judeo-Christian notion that the good first principle should purposefully make a material world and call it good was completely beyond them.

Among the Christians at this time, there was a rather large and influential tradition of skepticism about the value of science. Tertullian summarized this neatly when he said: "What does Athens have to do with Jerusalem?" Salvation is not through reason; therefore, one should flee reason, lest one not attain salvation. Faith alone saves us. Why waste time on philosophy?

There were, of course, Christians from the earliest times who held that faith and reason were compatible. St. Paul himself affirmed this when he wrote: "Ever since the creation of the world his invisible nature, namely, his eternal power and deity, has been clearly perceived from the things that have been made" (Romans 1:20, RSV). Here is the sanction for natural reason: one can learn of God the creator from the things of this world. Therefore, it is good to study the things of the world: science is good. Justin Martyr was an early member of this tradition, and St. Augustine is the great example, among the Fathers of the Church, of reason and faith working together.

In general, of those who were more philosophically minded, most early Christian thinkers tended to pick up the neo-Platonic philosophy with its tradition of suspicion, if not rejection, of the material world. This suspicion they thought in line with what the Scriptures teach. However, if, with Neoplatonism, one thinks that the material world is evil but that God is good, one finds oneself in a rather difficult situation. How can one explain the existence of the material world? God who is good could not have made the material world if it is evil. Therefore, there must be another creating being who is responsible for this mess. This way of explaining reality is known as dualism, and many of the early Christian philosophers fell prey to its doctrine. Instead of there being one good God who creates a completely good creation, there are two equally supreme forces, one the cause of immaterial things which are good, and the other the cause of the material world which is evil. That such a view is obviously not in line with the idea of there being one good creating cause of all things, they did not seem to notice. But holding such a view, they did not consider the material world to have the intrinsic value and permanence to warrant the attention that a legitimate and worthwhile scientific explanation would require. Even Augustine, who certainly did not fall into dualism as a result of his Neoplatonic philosophy, did tend to see the material world as of little importance. After all, the material world is constantly changing and passing away. God alone is unchanging, and thus God alone is really real. To spend one's time studying the not-quite-real is to be wasting one's time.

The modern mind, in general, embraces this antagonism of faith and reason under the influence of what we consider to be the great flowering of our western culture–the Renaissance and Reformation. From about the fifth century to about the fifteenth, there had grown up an intellectual tradition, known as scholasticism, which attempted to synthesize all knowledge. No truth was to be left out, regardless of whether it came from pagan philosophy or from Revelation. In this tradition, faith and reason were regarded not as antagonists but as allies. Philosophy was considered "the handmaid" of theology, and Revelation the guiding light of philosophy. What the thinkers of the Renaissance and Reformation did (not all, of course, but those the modern world recognizes–rightly or wrongly–as most significant) was to jettison this tradition. The Renaissance scientists, like Francis Bacon, did so in the name of progress, for they saw the Aristotelian elements of scholasticism as getting in the way of scientific progress. The Humanists, such as Erasmus, did so because they found the Latin style of the scholastics so unclassical, and the thought too technical. And the Reformers, such as Luther and Calvin, did so in the name of rejecting the Roman Church in whose fold the scholastics worked.

In actual fact, the Renaissance move to separate reason and faith was nothing new. This had largely been accomplished by many Catholic theologians of the late Middle Ages. Oddly enough, it seems to have been a theological movement which instigated the end of the partnership of faith and reason which had been such a

distinctly medieval achievement. In order to protect and
glorify the power of God, theologians began attributing
less and less real power to created things and especially to
the human mind. The order, causality, and meaning of
the world was gradually rolled back into God.

The battle cry of the Reformers is well-known. We are
saved by faith alone. The only truth is the truth of Christ;
no philosopher has ever spoken the truth. Therefore, we
must abandon philosophy if we would be saved. In the
more colorful language of Luther: "Philosophy is the
devil's whore."

As for natural reason, in which direction did it go? Although this is a vast simplification of a very complex issue,
let me venture to say that there were two main directions:
idealism and materialism.[1] These are not new positions to
us, for idealism is roughly what Plato and Neoplatonism
were up to, and materialism is the position of the Epicureans and Stoics. Both idealism and materialism are forms of
rationalism as defined in the last chapter; that is, both seek
to explain reality by presenting a coherent and complete
system of thought in which everything is accounted for
through a deduction of conclusions from axioms. Adherents to both idealism and materialism of this time agreed
in abandoning the scholastic tradition of synthesis which
held that our knowledge begins in sense experience but
rises to know immaterial realities and finally the truth that
God exists. However, this was about as far as they agreed.

Descartes exemplified idealism and began his explanation of reality with thought. From thought, he proved
that God exists. Finally, from our experience of thought
and knowledge of God, he proceeded to talk about the

---

[1]As used in this book, idealism refers to the philosophical position that
what is really real is immaterial and can be grasped by the mind alone.

material world. The only problem with this method is that from God and the mind it is extremely difficult to deduce information about the world. Hence, we find in Descartes, not so surprisingly, a rather sketchy and abstract physics. His disciples further emptied the material world of intrinsic meaning by developing a theory which had God doing everything and nature a mere facade for God's activity. This theory was known as "occasionalism" and its great exponent was a man by the name of Malebranche. On this view, fire, for example, does not really burn; rather, the proximity of the fire to my hand is the "occasion" for God to make my hand burn. All causality is rolled back into God. The absolute idealism of Bishop Berkeley made God the only source of our ideas about the world and completed the reduction of natural science to mind and then to God—the reduction of the creation to the creator. In a sense this tradition continued that train of thought begun in the late Middle Ages, namely, the attributing of all causality to God. This obviously spells the end of any science which studies the universe in itself.

Oddly enough, the other direction, materialism, also had its roots in late medieval theology. The idea that all we can know naturally are material things, and that our knowledge of them is really only a statistical probability based on repeated experiences, was not a brilliant new invention of the Renaissance scientific mind. The fourteenth-century theologian William of Ockham, eager to reserve all explanatory power for God, had said that all the common features and structures we think we recognize among the things of this world are not really there. This apple and that apple do not really share anything in common. You and I are not really the same at all; at least we cannot know that we are the same by natural reason.

Each thing is radically unique. Universal ideas, like "apple" and "human being," do not indicate any real community among the things they signify; they are just names which we find useful in organizing our intrinsically meaningless world. This theory which held ideas to be merely names was called "nominalism," from the Latin word for name, *nomen*. There can be no universal knowledge, only the endless, never-repeating, stream of raw data. The world is not ordered in itself: the order is merely in our minds in a rather shallow, fictitious sense, and in the mind of God in a real sense.

Now this way of thinking, if taken completely seriously, also spells the end of science as a legitimate inquiry into the structure of the universe. If scientists really do not consider there to be any structure in the world, then the process of hypothesis and verification that is the method of science makes no sense. If they do not believe that the world is ordered, then they are foolish to hypothesize about that order. Under conditions of strict nominalism, the whole project of science is absurd and should never be attempted. Of course the people of this tradition, such as the Renaissance scientist, Francis Bacon, did not stick to pure recording of data, but made use of hypotheses which they then set out to prove or disprove.

Thus, we have seen that either of these possible directions of trying to present a closed systematic explanation of the world (idealism or materialism), if followed exclusively, would make natural knowledge about the universe impossible. The emphasis on mind alone as source of all knowledge has no way to generate the material world which science investigates. The emphasis on matter alone can never generate any laws. To generate universal laws of matter, the two methods must be combined. The combination is what is called the scientific method: hypothesis verified by sense experience. Scientific method, however, although allowing for the exploration of the universe, still remains bound by the requirements of materialism. Verification of hypotheses must be a matter of physical information. The possibility of there being immaterial reality is ruled out from the start because it cannot be verified by the senses.

One thing the acceptance of materialism (carried on in the scientific method) did do, which is of particular interest to our discussion, was to make it impossible to know that God exists. If all that may be considered real must be able to be verified by sense experience, then the only real things are material. But God, the creator of the whole material universe, cannot be material. Therefore, according to materialism (and scientific method), God cannot be known to exist. One may believe in God, but then one's faith is held against all reasonable evidence. Such a faith is known as "fideism," and it really is the only faith option for the materialist or anyone who insists that the scientific method is the sole method for reaching truth. This tradition of materialism brought the status of faith and reason to what we sketched in the beginning of this chapter: faith and reason are separate spheres which do not overlap. Reason and its fruits (science) exclude faith along with all the things which apparently are of faith (such as the existence of God, creation, the immortal soul, etc.), and vice versa.

Of course, all this is vastly generalized, and there were many subtle positions other than those briefly sketched. But such a generalization is legitimate, I think, on two counts. In the first place, it sets up what really does appear to be a tension between the ideal of science and the notion of an all-powerful creating God. On the one hand, science strives to discover the necessary structures and order of the universe. If the universe is necessary, then there seems to be no need for a creator. Creation, on the other hand, is the free act of God; there are no constraints on God's action. If all is due to a cause which is unconstrained free will, then it would seem to follow that there is nothing necessary about the existence or structure of the universe. Secondly, this polarization of positions is, by and large, the way in which our world today sees the relationship between faith and reason, religion and science. It certainly seemed true to me, growing up in modern technological America, that what was required was a fundamental choice, or at best some kind of uneasy truce, between science and the notion of creation, and such is likely to be the attitude, on one level or another, of those of us raised under the banner of scientific progress and democratic ideals. Technology has delivered the goods; it gives us real things, bottom-line answers to what we need to survive, while metaphysics–we do not even know what the word means.[2] And even if we do, what good is metaphysics? How is it useful to us to know that the order of the universe points to an immaterial cause of everything? The answer is, of course, that it is not useful in the way technology is. But if one is interested in what is true, and in avoiding the entanglements of thought and action that result from muddle-headedness, then metaphysics cannot be ignored. I hope the vital importance of metaphysics will become clear in the course of this book.

---

[2]Literally, metaphysics means "beyond physics." Classical metaphysics studies what is real, and this study culminates in the consideration of immaterial (nonphysical) beings as providing ultimate answers. But Bacon, for example, considered metaphysics equivalent to superstition, and we often use the term today to mean unimportant: "that problem is purely metaphysical," meaning it is not a problem at all.

From what has been said, then, it appears that to hold both positions–that the universe is created but also the appropriate subject of scientific investigation–is to involve oneself in a contradiction. Thomas Aquinas held both, and not as uneasy bedfellows, but as mutually supportive foundations of the human quest to understand reality. Let us now discuss in more detail the pieces of the puzzle and how Aquinas fit them together.

Since the radical philosophical breakthrough of Aquinas was his doctrine of creation, let us begin with that pole of the paradox. As I said, Plato and Aristotle and the Greek philosophical tradition in general never dreamed of saying that the world was created. The world had its first necessary causes and the like, but none was ever considered the cause of the totality of existing things. The universe has always been. There are first causes within the universe to explain what it is like, but no cause of the universe, to explain that it is as opposed to there being nothing at all.

The question that was central to the Greek philosophical debates was the question "what is change?" It seems obvious that things do change (although one Greek philosopher, Parmenides, denied it), but how come? Change is not self-explanatory, for it is a transition over time from one state or place to another. What accounts for it leaving the first state and approaching the second? It surely cannot be the original state itself, for that is limited in its actuality to what it is prior to the change. Let us take a couple of examples. It is impossible for water at fifty degrees Fahrenheit to raise its own temperature to the boiling point. The flag does not cause itself to wave. Change requires a cause–eventually, as Plato and Aristotle understood, one that is not itself changing. Without some unchanging first cause, the present observable case of change would have no ultimate explanation. If the cause of this change is itself changing, then it requires a cause of its change. But there cannot be an infinite series of causes. Ultimately, change is explained only by reference to an unchanging cause.

I must call your attention here to one very important point, which is absolutely critical to understanding metaphysics (which is the only way to prove that God exists). When Aristotle and Aquinas say that there cannot be an infinite number of causes one depending on another, they do not mean causes in a temporal series, such as one billiard ball setting another in motion, or one man being the father of another. The causal series which cannot be infinite, which must have a first cause, is the hierarchical one of causes operating simultaneously. In such a series, the observed change and the ultimate unchanging cause (and any other changing causes in between) are all operating at the same time. Metaphysics is concerned with the immediate dependence of one thing on another at this moment and in this moment. The dependence is not one of horizontal before and after, but of vertical hierarchy–one thing depending immediately on another kind of thing. Metaphysics differs from physics not only in being concerned with the immaterial in the final analysis, but also in being concerned with relations of a moment, as opposed to causality stretched out in time. Thus, the creation that metaphysics proves has nothing to do with whether there was a Big Bang and anything before it or not; rather, metaphysics proves that everything at this moment and at every moment depends on a creating cause for its existence.

Let me present an example which I think will help explain what kind of causal structure metaphysics considers. I am fishing, and I get a trout on the line. There are two ways of explaining why I am catching the fish. You may say, on the one hand, that my history is such that it has led to this moment, and that my history is traceable back to my father, grandfather, etc., back to the beginnings of human life, back through the chain of evolution, back through cosmic time to the Big Bang, and whatever came before it (if something did). This is cause and effect in a temporal line, a line of explanation a scientist might use to tell me how I came to be catching a fish at this moment: to find out why anything is so, see what came before.

But there is another way of explaining why I am catching the fish, which involves a chain of causality which operates in simultaneous dependence. My catching the fish depends on the fly the fish has in its mouth. However, this is not a sufficient explanation. Without the line attached to the fly, the fly would not do me much good. So my catching the fish depends on the fly which depends on the line. The chain of causality travels back (not in time, but dependence) to the rod, my hand, my arm, my body, my muscles, my neural structure, my knowledge of how to fish, and finally to my free will choice to go fishing. Here we have reached the first cause in this series.[3] Catching the fish depends on all the causes we mentioned in a hierarchical order of dependence. If any cause were to fail, the fish would not be caught. And without the first uncaused cause, that is, my decision to fish, the activity would not happen at all. But the activity is happening; therefore, that first cause is operating. In this kind of causality, if one takes away the cause, the effect vanishes. This is obviously quite unlike the temporal causal series, in which the removal of the cause is not the removal of the effect. If I pick up the cue ball immediately after my shot,

---

[3]In actual fact, my own free will choice is itself caused, and hence one can continue the causal chain until it discovers God the creator; but this is a topic for Chapter Four.

this does not stop the motion of the eight ball which missed the pocket and continues to ricochet off the various bumpers. The fact that yesterday is no more does not take away today, and my grandfather's death does not necessitate my father's death or my own.

Both kinds of causal relationships are legitimate ways of looking at the world. The only causal structure of dependence in coming to be which the natural sciences consider is the temporal one, for what is real is presupposed by the scientific method to be material, and no two material things can operate simultaneously in the same place. The relationship which is of simultaneous dependence is the one metaphysics considers, and this kind of relationship is the only way to show that God the creator exists.

This metaphysical way of thinking was what Plato and Aristotle were about when they said that change requires an unchanging cause. Without an ultimate cause, there can be no derivative causes or effects; but there is change: therefore there is a first changeless cause. There may, in fact, be more than one unchanging cause, since there are many effects to be explained, not all alike. Plato explained this world of changing things by saying these things were trying to imitate fixed and perfect patterns. There are two poles of reality, being and non-being, and changing things are in between, in the halfway house of becoming. The physical tree we meet is not "tree" in the full sense, but rather participates in, or imitates, the perfect nonphysical paradigm of tree as best it can. Aristotle's answer for explaining change was to say that there is an unmoved mover which is perfect and, as perfect, acts as an object of love which all imperfect things seek insofar as they seek their own perfection. All change is caused by something which is actual in a way that the changing thing is not. For example, an oak sapling in its growing can be said to be seeking the perfection of a mature oak. Human beings in trying to know can be said to seek the perfection of all-knowingness. Even a stone rolling off a cliff can be said to be seeking its perfect place–the actual center of the gravitational field in which it exists, which is the center of the earth. In general, all things naturally seek their own perfection. Since this seeking is an instance of change, and all change requires an unchanging first cause, there must exist an unchanging, fully-actual, perfect being which is the ultimate cause of absolutely all change in the world.

These ultimate, unchanging beings of Plato and Aristotle are necessary: they cannot fail to be and have always been. This, they figured, was the end of the explanation. The world just is and has always been. Plato and Aristotle explained this realm of changing material things by saying that there are immaterial, unchanging things which cause these things to change.

Thomas Aquinas took the principles and arguments of Plato and Aristotle and pushed them one more step, not violating the principles, nor denying the arguments as far as they went, but showing that the principles and arguments revealed more about the universe than his Greek predecessors had known. Aquinas's argument goes something like this. We find ourselves confronted by things other than ourselves, and we ask "Why?" Why are these things what they are, and why are they here? We formulate answers and test them for correctness and completeness. We naturally want to know, and sometimes the first answers we receive are not sufficient to quell our desire to know. So again we ask why, only this time on a deeper level. The remainder that is left over after the explanation has been given (the questioning voice that is unsatisfied) impels us on our quest for deeper, more comprehensive, knowledge. We recognize a question, and seek an answer.

This is what philosophy (and for that matter, science) is all about. The last remainder, the frontier question which remains whatever explanation has been given from within this universe–the question "Why is there a universe at all and not nothing?"–this is the question of creation, to which the answer is God the creator.

This has been much too quick and abstract. Let us run through the case for a creating God a couple of more times using different examples. Questions arise in specific situations, about specific things. A question is centered on one thing or group of things in the context of others. The world of our experience is irreducibly plural, and the existence of many things that are different is what impels us to ask "how come?" and to continue to ask this on deeper and deeper levels until no further questions arise. Take anything in one's field of experience, this dog Spot, for example. To the question "How come Spot?" there are many answers which can be given. (Notice that we are beginning with a material thing, one to which our access is easy and immediate.) On a first level one may answer the question by identifying Spot's parents. If one is merely mildly curious of the pet's beginnings, then this answer may satisfy, for it would specify Spot as an individual dog. But suppose one is interested in classifying dogs or animals in general. Then the answer might be that Spot is a spaniel and not a beagle, or that he is a dog and not a pig or a porcupine. Maybe one is a biologist and is interested in what makes things alive. One might then classify Spot among living things. Each question reaches more deeply into the broad structures of reality and attempts to give a more comprehensive answer in terms of a larger context of reality. On an even deeper, more universal, level, one might explain Spot chemically. The deepest level known to modern science is on the level of physics. One might explain the existence of Spot by giving an account of the general laws of physics. Here we have a structure of universality which is common to all material things that belong to this spacio-temporal order. Yet there is an explanation deeper than even the basic structuring principles of physics. On the deepest and most general level of all, one might reply to the question "How come Spot?" by answering: "Because there is anything at all, and not nothing." It is conceivable that there be nothing, and so the question "How come?" read in this way is legitimate. Some may not have raised this question consciously, but that is no reason to reject it as a legitimate question. Some have not raised the question of the chemical content of Spot, or even the question of his breed, yet these questions are surely legitimate.

Is it because we have no answer for this question that we are prone to reject it? If so, then we ought to reject all questions, for questions are only about things for which we have no answer. We only proceed to the next deeper level of the search for knowledge because something remains unexplained. Explanation in itself does not push us deeper; it is what is still unclear that is the catalyst for further exploration. Spot exists because his parents are Fred and Lulu. Yes, but how come Spot has fluffy ears and a waggy tale and not a curlicue tail or sharp quills. He's a dog. Fine, but how come he eats and breathes and sleeps? He's a living thing as opposed to inanimate. O.K., but how do we explain that. There is the answer in terms of chemical constitution. Deeper still is the more universally comprehensive answer of physics: he's made of such and such primary particles obeying such and such fundamental laws of all matter and energy. Yes, but why is there a universe? The answer to this question, one which we know we cannot comprehend, is God the creator. The reason we cannot comprehend the answer is because to do so we would have to define the cause in question, and that would mean placing God the creator in the context of other things. However, as the cause of all things, the creator does not exist as one among other things; he does not share a world with the things he has created.

Let me try another analogy which, at the risk of over-simplifying, may offer a helpful image as a beginning. Analogies are only beginnings which must be thought through and beyond. They are helpful images, but images are not thoughts. All analogies fail to communicate adequately the idea in question, and this is how it must be, since an analogy attempts to make something unknown or little known clearer by comparing it with something better known. What I want to do is to give a spatial analogy for the dependence in being of any one thing (like Spot) on the ultimate ground which is God the creator.

Imagine yourself in Egypt, gazing at a pyramid. Focus on the capstone. How does one account for the position of that particular stone? In the first place it rests on the broader base of the stones on the level beneath it. The position of these, in turn, is explained by the next broader level. This broadening of base is analogous to the deepening levels of explanation which science gives of things within the universe. Let the procedure go on until we have explained the shape and order of the pyramid (like science explaining the universe). When all this has been explained, we may answer the question as to why the capstone is where it is on yet a deeper level by saying that the ultimate explanation of the capstone's position is the earth on which the pyramid stands. Nothing within the shape and structure of the pyramid can guarantee that the pyramid has anything on which to stand. Likewise, nothing within the universe, no necessary forces no matter how universal, can guarantee that there be a universe to be so structured. As the earth makes possible the chain of positional causality which underlies the capstone, so God the creator makes possible the order of the universe which underlies any particular existing thing.

Having read an interpretation and discussion of what I hold to be the central insight in Aquinas's metaphysics, the place where he surely goes beyond his illustrious Greek predecessors, the reader may be interested to know what Aquinas himself said on the subject. I shall quote but one passage here. "When we speak of the production of some particular creature, we are able to assign the reason why it is such a thing from other creatures, or at least from the order of the universe, to which every creature is ordered as a part to the form of the whole. When, however we speak of the whole universe being called forth into existence, we are not able to find anything created from which the reason why it is such and such can be taken."[4] There are causes within the universe to explain what things are, and these causes are on many levels of universality, from the most specific (Spot's parents) to the most universal (the general laws of physics). None of these, however, can explain why there is a universe, why there is anything at all and not nothing. The answer to this puzzle, which is the ultimate question about reality, is God the creator.

The reason the ancient Greeks held fast against any notion of something being made from nothing was that the only kind of making they could imagine was change. For a flower to come to be, there must be a seed; for summer to come to be, there must be a change in the positions of

---

[4]Thomas Aquinas, *De Potentia Dei* III, 17; all translations from the Latin are my own.

the heavenly bodies; for a human being to come to be, there must be other human beings as parents, whose sexual union begins a process which issues in a child's birth. Some of the Greeks did have a notion of universes coming to be, but this is not creation. The universes always came to be out of something else–fire, or the undifferentiated, or chaos, or something of the sort. In short, they had the notion of cycles of destruction and reformation of reality, but never the notion of the coming to be of the entire universe from nothing. And in some ways it is small wonder, for creation from nothing is impossible to imagine. Imagination requires images, and images are spatio-temporal. Therefore, to imagine the universe coming to be, one must picture it coming to be from something else, and for the imagination this something else must be material. So when the notion of creation from nothing presents itself to the human mind, the mind is profoundly puzzled. What could creation be like? The truth is it is not like anything else one has ever experienced. It is not in relation to other things; it is the relation of all things to the cause of all things. This means that God is not a thing as we understand the term. God, as we can know him, does not have an essence which we can define in relation to other things, except for saying that God is infinite (in power, goodness, truth), eternal, uncaused–all ways of saying that God is not like anything we know or imagine. For this reason, Aquinas is fond of saying that God is not really related to things, although they are really related to him. The easiest way of understanding this is to say that all things really do depend on God but he in no way depends on them.

Creation, thus, is a matter of dependence. As a philosophical doctrine based on natural reason, it does not and cannot claim that the universe was created at a first moment of time. Aquinas freely admits that it cannot be

proven that God created at a first moment of time. However, this does not deny that God is creator. The universe
at all times, whether time be infinite (as Aristotle and the
Greeks thought) or finite (as Jews and Christians believe),
depends on God for its very existence. Aquinas uses the
word conservation to help make this important point
clearer to us. Lest we misunderstand creation as one act of
God in the past, Aquinas says that God the creator conserves all things in existence. Actually, creation and conservation are really the same thing. But from our point of
view creation as Aquinas means it looks like conservation:
things continue to be created from moment to moment.
God himself, as we have mentioned and will discuss more
in Chapter Four, is not in time, and so creation from his
point of view is not from moment to moment but all at
once. God creates all things, including time. His perfect
simplicity as first cause means that the composition of
temporal succession cannot belong to him.

Where does this bring us concerning the things of the
world? Are they emptied of any reality of their own, depending as they do on God for everything? It might indeed appear so, for all the intelligibility and activities of
created things must preexist in the creator if he is to create
them. If we say that the whole of what things are preex-
ists in God, does this mean that there is nothing real in
creatures? Indeed, it might appear that in learning that
God the creator exists, we have emptied the universe of
intrinsic meaning. But this is not true. To say that something exists is not to say what it is. Aquinas is very consistent in saying that we do not and cannot know God's nature by natural reason. This is because God is infinite and
a finite mind cannot understand an infinite being. When
we know something to exist from its effects, and not from

direct experience of it, then the best we can do is say what that thing cannot be, and what it minimally must be if it is the cause of the effects: for example, God must be knowing and have free will since he is the cause of human beings who know and will. Even so, we do not know what God's knowing and free will are like. If we could know God's nature as well as knowing that he is the cause of all things, then we could deduce the universe and all its intricacies directly from him. As it is, all we know of God we glean from the things that are the immediate objects of our experience. God does not give answers to the world (not in the philosophical order, anyway). Therefore, it is not true that in knowing God (in the sense of knowing that he exists) we know the world (in the sense of knowing what it is). And thus, the doctrine of creation is not a replacement for science. Science, with its search for and discovery of the necessary aspects of the universe is, in fact, precisely what leads us to the notion of God the creator. Let us explore this surprising truth in some more depth.

What kind of things does Aquinas say are necessary, and more basically, as we begin, what does he mean by necessary? Aquinas defines "necessary being" the same way that Aristotle does: it is a being which cannot be corrupted (cease being what it is) by any process of nature. The opposite of necessary being is "contingent being"–a thing which can be corrupted by processes of nature, such as a flower, bird, a chemical compound, or even an atom (the human action of nuclear fission counts as a natural process). To be necessary or contingent has nothing to do with whether a thing is created or not. All things are caused to exist by God: this means necessary as well as contingent things.

What we are concerned with here is the nature of things, and that cannot be learned from knowing that the world is created. To be created, although it makes all the difference to a thing in making it be at all, adds nothing to the nature of a thing. If it did, no kind of thing could be created. If tree plus being created gives one something besides tree, then God could never create a tree. Every time he tried, he would get, not a tree, but a tree-plus-something-else. If we want to know whether or not there are any necessary beings, we cannot study God and his activity which is creation: we must study the world.

When the puzzle of contingency (that there are things which exist but need not exist, and in fact are passing away) sets us wondering, the procedure of looking for the reason for the actual existence of what might not have been leads us to the discovery that there are things in the world which must necessarily exist. These things which must be are, if you will, the unchanging laws of coming to be. Aquinas and Aristotle called these necessary beings "separate substances." On their model of cosmology, the separate substances cause the heavens to move in ways which cause things to come into being. Modern science is more sophisticated in its analysis and talks of the four great forces in the universe: gravity, electromagnetism, the strong force, and the weak force. Both of these scientific world views recognize that there must be necessary features of the universe if there are contingent features, for what only has the potential for being cannot make itself be. For things to come to be now, there must be some actual and necessary cause acting now. All unexplained features of this world, whether change or the present existence of contingent things, require a cause that is not subject to the question-raising incompleteness of the changing or contingent thing. Only an unchanging, necessary being raises no further questions (except, of course, the question of its existence, which is the question of creation). So the first things that Aquinas says are naturally necessary are the fundamental laws of the universe.

Besides these, there are features of the universe whose activities transcend time and which therefore must also be necessary. These are, to the surprise of most modern readers who have grown up in the shadow of behaviorism and computer models, ourselves in our ability to think. To know is to be engaged in an activity that gets beyond the here and now. Two plus two equals four; a frog is not a mountain; the law of gravity obtains for all matter: these are statements that are true for all times and all places. An immaterial activity can only be performed by an immaterial faculty. Thus, the rational soul is immaterial and as immaterial is not subject to corruption. The rational souls of all the human beings that have ever been are thus permanent and necessary features of the universe.[5] Lastly, Aquinas says that the universe itself is necessary. Hold on a minute. Didn't we just say that the universe depends on God, and that therefore it might not be? Yes, but the fact that the universe depends on God has nothing to do with its necessity or contingency. God is the cause of all things; and things are necessary or contingent. The question of a thing's necessity or contingency has nothing to do with its being created. Its nature is necessary or contingent; the fact that it exists at all is due to God. So if there is evidence available to natural reason which says that the universe is necessary and therefore permanent, then it is correct to say that the universe is necessary. Two aspects of the universe have been seen to be necessary: the funda-

---

[5]To what extent the indestructibility of the rational soul means the indestructibility of the human being will be discussed in the next chapter.

mental laws of all coming to be, and human minds. In addition to these, Aquinas says that the totality of physical things is also necessary. Since there is nothing physical outside the totality of physical things, there can be nothing into which the physical universe could change, nothing which could underlie the change or serve as a transitional material, and nothing which could cause the change.

To make this last point clear, let us consider an example of what Aquinas calls "substantial" change–the changing of one thing into another. What is required for grass to change into cow? In the first place, there must be something besides grass in the universe–cow, for instance. Secondly, there must be something that can underlie the change from grass to cow–chemical and molecular structures. Finally, there must be something to initiate the change–hungry cow. But when we look for things to fulfill these functions in terms of the whole physical universe becoming something else, we can find none. Grass is one physical thing; the universe is every physical thing. The structure of amino acids is one principle of continuity which can underlie change; but there is nothing in common between being and non-being. A cow is a different kind of actual thing than grass; but non-being is not a different kind of thing from the universe of existing things: it is nothing at all.

God, of course, could annihilate the universe, but this would not be a change (just as creation is not a change) and it would not be natural, but supernatural. The important point is that there is nothing in the nature of the universe which indicates that the universe as a whole can cease to exist. The fundamental forces (whatever they may be) are necessary and therefore permanent; immaterial things like minds are necessary and therefore also permanent; and the material universe as a whole is necessary and hence permanent. Add them up and one has covered all the things that are: and none is naturally capable of returning to nothing. It is time for another quote from the master himself. "In all created nature, there is no potency by which it is possible for something to tend toward nothingness."[6] And so science is quite right in attributing necessity to the universe.

But far from this discounting the fact that the world is created, it is the very discovery of necessity in the universe that causes us to go beyond the universe for its radical cause of existence. It is not until we have exhausted the answers to the question "why?" which are available within the universe (that is, not until we have reached the fundamental laws of nature) that our question turns to the totality of being. It is the irreducible plurality of necessary things that raises for us the further question of why these necessary things should exist. Consider the fundamental laws of physics. At present scientists tell us that there are four. Now these necessary laws are different, or there would not be four, yet it is true of all of them that they exist necessarily. What is unique to each cannot be the cause of what is common to all. Therefore, there must be a universal cause of their being necessary; this is God the creator. The cause cannot be another distinct kind of necessary being, since to be necessary is to escape dependence on some other kind of thing within the universe.

Perhaps, one might say, science will some day succeed in reducing the four laws to one fundamental law. Even then, it will still be true that there will be two irreducible things: the material universe which this law explains and

---

[6]*De Potentia Dei* V, 3.

the mind that knows it. To know such a universal law, the mind must transcend the material universe, for matter is always particular and changeable. Thus, there are at least two necessary things (and many more when one counts other human minds) which differ in what they are but agree in the fact that they exist necessarily. Since neither the physical universe nor the human intellect can explain their shared necessary existence, there must be a common cause of necessary existence (and hence of all existence), and this is God the creator.

God the creator is not the end of scientific inquiry, but the permanently open question which invites the mind's search for meaning, which, as search, is always into the unknown–into mystery. The question of creation is the lifeblood of scientific progress, not its death knell. God has given things existence, and like all gifts (something that comes freely and undeserved) God's gift of being to all things is permanent. The universe is really real. It is not that it is theoretically impossible for God to annihilate the universe: since everything depends on God at every moment, he would merely have to cease sustaining the universe in being and it would return to nothingness. But there is no reason to think that this will happen, but, on the contrary, reasons to believe that he will not annihilate the world. God did not grant being to a world that he thought deserved it, on the condition that later on, if he thought that the world no longer deserved to exist, he would destroy it. There is no "later on" for God. God is perfectly simple, unchangeable, eternal. God does not change his mind: he has no need to since nothing, as it

were, talks back to God.[7] Thus, no new information might
come to God that would cause him to change his mind.
There could be nothing conditional about God granting
existence to things since before God's gift there was
nothing to demand the condition. In no sense can God be
said to owe existence to things, which responsibility he
might at some time want to duck. Thus, his decision to
create is fully free and independent of any thing; and it is
fully wise, for God comprehends the totality of existence,
the whole of time. Nor can God grow tired of sustaining
the world, and so the world be destroyed because God
falls asleep or suffers a momentary lapse of attention. God
is pure activity (the requirement to be first cause). Of
course we cannot imagine or conceive of what pure activity means, but we know that God is the first cause of all
things, and that if he were in any way potential, then he
could be actualized by another, and thus would not be the
first cause. He would not be what we mean by God the
creator of all things, but rather a limited thing among
other limited things. The God who is pure activity cannot
be made more actual; he cannot receive help, nor does he
need any. And so, from all that we can know about the
universe and God, there is no indication that the universe
will revert to nothing. It is a permanent creation.

We have shown that knowing God to be the creator does
not do away with our need to investigate nature through
science and the propriety of this investigation. Is the pursuit of science a barrier to knowing God the creator?
While it is true to say that creation is the great guarantor
of nature and instigator of scientific exploration, this is not
in any way at the expense of denigrating God's power.

---

[7]The rebellion that is sin does not in any way harm God: it only harms
the sinner–but this is for Chapter Five.

The movement in the late Middle Ages which took away from nature to magnify the creator was profoundly mistaken. The more ordered is the creation, the more reason to wonder at the power and wisdom of the creator. It is much greater achievement to write a play like Shakespeare's *Macbeth* or *King Lear* in which characters and events take on real life of their own, than it is to write a play where the author is always showing up to manipulate events and people. In the same way, the fact that God has created a world with its own intrinsic causality, one in which he is not an alternative or intruder, is much more glorious than for him to make a world which he dangles on a string like a puppeteer. The fear which some believers in God have of science is thus unfounded, and might in fact end up steering them away from the true God. For the notion of God as manipulating and abrogating at will the laws of nature casts God in the role of strongest power within the universe. But such a notion limits God, making him a thing among other things. To worship such a God is to worship part of the universe, is to worship an idol.

My point here is not to venture into theology and faith, but to dispel any notion that hard thinking destroys faith. Natural reason, far from being an enemy of faith is its protector. This is one point of which Aquinas was absolutely convinced. Since both nature and Revelation come from the same source, and the source is all wise and all good, they cannot contradict one another. If this book has any direct relation to faith, it is but to show that faith is not contrary to reason. It is true that faith is not the culmination of natural reason, for faith is a supernatural gift from God; but neither does reason counsel against faith. One can know through reason that there is a cause of everything, which means a cause of one's every action, and of every event. Knowing this, it surely is not unreasonable to commit oneself to the source of all being, activity, and meaning, even if the commitment is to something beyond one's comprehension. The commitment is to mystery, that is, uncharted meaning. Reason brings one to the threshold of a new relationship with the source of all being. Whether one accepts the invitation to love this being or not is a matter of grace, but the acceptance could not be called unreasonable, for it is not made against the requirements of reason.

Aquinas says often that grace does not destroy nature, but brings it to perfection. Thus, a life informed by faith is not unnatural. God is not an alternative to nature. His actions do not disrupt or interfere with nature. One could just as well, it seems to me, say with Aquinas that nature does not preclude grace, but opens up to it. In other words, grace is not unnatural. Because God is the cause of nature and thus not part of nature, his entering nature does not mean disruption. Disruption comes about when some one kind of thing interferes with the activity of some other kind of thing. But God is not a kind of thing such that his activity is an alternative to any other activity. In fact, his activity, as the cause of all other activity, cannot be contradictory to any.

This is an extremely difficult notion to grasp. In all our experience of nature, when one thing acts on another the other's action is distorted in some way. When the sun shines and the rain does not come, the grass turns brown and the spinach withers. When the spider catches the fly in its net and proceeds to deal with it, the fly's normal activity is distorted and devoured. If I hypnotize you, you do as I say and not as you would freely choose. But the same is not true of God's activity in the world. Since God is not any thing, but the creator of all things, his presence to the world need not alter it. In fact, God's absence to it is what would alter it–not, indeed, into something else, but back into nothingness.

So one sees that what Aquinas understood was that these two apparently antagonistic positions–that the world depends radically on a creating God, and that science discovers necessity in the world–are not mutually exclusive. The pursuit of science leads us to the question of God the creator. If one asks the fundamental scientific question "Why?" persistently and uncompromisingly, one comes to ask the question about the entire universe of things as over against nothing. Now it is true that the answer we give to such a question, i.e., God the creator, is not subject to verification by the senses, and hence falls outside scientific method.[8] Thus, there is no scientific answer to our question, for it is a question not about how the physical world operates (a matter of physics) but rather about the existence itself of the universe (a matter of metaphysics). The point is that scientific method is the proper one for biology, chemistry, astronomy, and physics, but it is not the only method for achieving truth. It cannot deal with questions about immaterial realities such as God or, more immediately, the human mind itself which knows universal and unchanging realities and hence cannot itself be bound to the particular flux of matter (the very mind that does science); and, as we shall see in Chapter Five, scientific method cannot deal with ethical matters, with issues of what one ought to do, that is, with universal obligation.

The question "Why?" is thus a question that, while science asks it, properly transcends all specific methods. It is a human question, which indicates the fundamental desire

---

[8]But note that the presupposition that scientific method is the only valid way of establishing truth itself falls outside sense verification.

to know which is essential to all human beings. It is not a question asked on condition that one knows that there is a comprehensive answer to it. Such a question would not really be a question at all. The question of God is pure question, pure quest for meaning. Not only does science lead us to the question of God, but the question of God in turn supports the scientific quest for intelligibility. To say that God is creator is in no way to repeal or trivialize the work of science; on the contrary it is to validate and encourage the scientific quest. God creates a world of real things, not a facade behind which he alone operates. The only way we can know God naturally is through the things he has made. Therefore, the question of what God is, which we ask persistently though never formulating an adequate answer, steers us directly to the things which require his existence in order that they be what they are. To know the perfections of things, which knowledge we gain through natural channels, is the best and really the only way we have of knowing what God is like or, more precisely, of excluding errors about God. To know that all things are created will not tell one about what things are, but it will tell one that they have a single source of being and meaning. This piece of news is good news indeed to the scientific quest which seeks to understand the world as a whole.

When all this has been said, one may still be puzzled as to how the universe can be necessary and permanent while depending completely on a single creating cause. But it should be clear, at least, that the puzzlement is not due to a defect in reason, but rather to the great success of reason in bringing one to deeper meaning. The world is a much stranger place than we first thought. Reason, instead of deadening our interest in the world ("now that we have all the answers, who cares"), kindles the wonder that is the life of the mind. Meaning is not narrowed to an either/or. Reason, properly followed, does not end in the absurdity of denying one truth in favor of another, but flowers into wonder at the mystery that is our being here in this world. Aquinas's understanding of God as creator is the fruit of a both/and attitude toward the truth. Wherever truth is found, it is to be embraced. It is never right to abandon truth just because one cannot see how to fit it in one's system or way of thinking. If one holds to the truth, which may, as in this case, be a dynamic relation between two apparent antagonists, then what happens is that one's system changes, one's story changes, and one transcends the partial in a fuller understanding. This is the story of science, of Ptolemy, Galileo, Newton, Einstein and beyond; and it is the story of human beings growing into the life of the mind which, far from being a dead end of "last words" and "bottom lines," turns out to be the open-ended adventure of reason into wonder. Our search for meaning leads to mystery, that is, ever-deeper and richer meaning.

III

The Mysterious Unity of the Human Being

Besides introducing the radical notion of creation in full force to the philosophical tradition, Thomas Aquinas also presented a radical philosophical position on the what is to be a human being. When I say radical, I do not mean revolutionary in the sense that Aquinas invented a brand new position without roots in his predecessors. On the contrary, it was Aquinas's insistence that the truth of the tradition be upheld that led him to his new position. Whenever truth is met, it is to be cherished and protected. In this sense, Aquinas's positions are very literally radical, for he worked on the roots of the problem.[1] He did not cut off branches of the old tree of knowledge hoping to make a whole new tree as did many of the philosophers of the modern tradition. Rather, he sought deeper in the old

---

[1]The word "radical" comes from the Latin *radix*, which means root.

tradition of wisdom and found that the diverse branches were rooted in a deeper unity that his predecessors had not seen.

Like the problem of understanding the world, there is a problem in understanding what it means to be human. Of all the material things in the world, only human beings think; and of all thinking beings, only human beings are material. There are two common ways of trying to deal with this odd fact. The one seeks to explain thinking in terms of matter and hence to dissolve the dilemma by denying the uniqueness of thought. The other seeks to explain matter in terms of thought, thereby solving the problem by saying that what is really the human being is what does the thinking, i.e., the rational soul, and that the body is not really me. There are, of course, variations on these themes, but these are the most obvious ways of responding to the problem, and they seem to have been held by some philosophers at all times.

Let us begin by considering the position that human beings are only matter. We mentioned a couple of ancient forms of materialism in the last chapter: Epicureanism and Stoicism. To these should be added the position known as atomism which held that reality is composed of tiny un-splittable bits of matter moving in a void. Besides these roots in the ancient world, materialism is also a typically modern position, espoused in different ways by many philosophers of the Renaissance and Enlightenment, such as Francis Bacon, Thomas Hobbes, and David Hume. It is also widely held today by those who believe that scientific method, with its insistence that what is real be verifiable by sense experience in experiment, is the only way of obtaining truth about the things of the world.[2]

Materialism, as a theory of human nature, grows out of the immediate conviction that we are bodies in relationship with other material things. This piece of evidence seems too obvious to require proof. It is simply commonsensical to say that the human being is material. One is born of certain parents at a certain place and time. One requires food and drink to live. One is bitten by mosquitoes and may be harmed or killed by weapons or disease. Thus, from direct evidence, it seems absolutely certain that we are made of matter; and indirect evidence also seems to support this claim, for it is impossible to imagine an immaterial thing. In the face of these two evidences, what reason would one have for doubting that materialism holds the only explanation of what it is to be human?

The reason lies precisely in explanation. To explain is to appeal to something immaterial, something which transcends the particular materiality of the thing explained –and the explainer and explainee, as well. Any astronomer will tell you that the earth is not a sphere, for its surface is not equidistant in all places from a central point. As a matter of fact, there never has nor could exist a perfect sphere in the material universe. But we know what a sphere is. Therefore, knowledge of geometry (and mathematics in general) is not explainable by material things alone. Consider another example. If I explain to you that a particular animal under discussion cannot be an eagle because it lacks wings and has a hard shell, I am ap-

---

[2]Contemporary physics speaks more of energy than of bits of matter, but it still holds to the ultimate requirement of some possible sense experience as verification of what is real, which effectively rules out the things traditionally held to be immaterial-- i.e., God, the rational soul, absolute moral norms.

pealing to objective criteria which are true about the differences between eagles and turtles, whenever and wherever they may be found. While individual material things
themselves always exist at particular times and places,
explanations about the differences between them are
always universal and true across time and place.
Therefore, explanation is not material. Another way of
saying the same thing is to say that meaning is immaterial.
If it were material, it could not be both in my mind and in
yours simultaneously.

In short, materialists neglect what they are doing when
they formulate their position: they fail to pay attention to
the fact that they are thinking. Unlike sensing which is
always in response to a particular material object, thinking
is about what is common to more than one thing. If we
recognize that two things are alike, then this recognition is
of what is common or universal. What is known to make
them alike is not itself material; if it were, it could not be
known to be in each in the same way, since material
things are here and not there, now and not then.

Let us consider another example. Say we are presented
with two wagging, barking animals, one of which is two
feet long, sleek, ankle high, and looks like a hot dog while
the other is five feet long, bushy, stands to one's waist,
and looks like a gigantic traveling dust mop. We look at
them both, think about them, and pronounce that they are
a couple of dogs, one a dachshund and the other an Eng-
lish sheep dog. They do not look much the same, nor
measure the same, nor feel the same: nevertheless we understand that they are the same in some fundamental
ways. They are both alive and moving; they both wag
their tails when supper comes, and they both bark at
strangers. They are animals, and more specifically, dogs.
Our senses recognize mostly differences; from what our

senses gather in, our minds focus on what is common. This common element of "dogginess" is not itself a material thing because it can be applied across time and space. It applies to wagging, barking animals yesterday and today, in Idaho and Peking. Aquinas explains this process of coming to understand, which he calls abstraction, in this way: "The intellect, according to its very nature, is altogether elevated above matter: this is shown by its operation, for we understand something only by separating it from matter."[3]

It is true that sensation precedes and imagination accompanies all our acts of knowing, but the essential object of knowing, that feature which distinguishes it from sensing or imagining is immaterial. Only if this is true can there be explanation. In fact, we reject an explanation unless it has the kind of universality which rises above the senses and the imagination. "You're dreaming. You just imagined that. Are you blind?" All these are rejections of the sufficiency of sensation and imagination for explanation. Communication of meaning is only possible because what is understood is in both minds at once, an impossibility for anything material. Thus, what is understood must be immaterial.

How can an immaterial object be known? It cannot be known by the senses or the imagination, which are bodily activities, for one of the foundations for materialism (one which even those who disagree with materialism would accept) is that immaterial things cannot be verified by the senses or imagination. Since we do know some things that cannot be sensed or imagined, such as the definition of a circle, or the distinction between a mountain and a valley, or the fact that all material things take up space, we

[3] *Compendium Theologiae*, 84.

must know them through the use of some immaterial component of our being. This immaterial component is usually referred to as the mind or intellect.

Since this is such an important point, let us present just one more way of showing that the mind or intellect must be immaterial. As we said above, to know something is to grasp what is essential about it, what makes it be the kind of thing that it is. In understanding what something is, one holds the nature of the thing in one's mind apart from its particular materiality. As Aristotle said, to know something is to be, in a way, the thing that is known. It is to have that thing existing mentally in oneself. This is the unique characteristic of being a knower: one can be not only oneself, but other things as well, to the extent that one knows what other things are. Now on the model of knowing as a material process, this could not happen; for if our sharing in the nature of some other thing were a physical sharing, then upon knowing, we would cease to be what we are and become that other thing. This is the kind of exchange of natures that happens among other material things all the time. When grass comes to share in the nature of cow, the grass ceases to be what it was and becomes cow. The communication of nature is of a material kind, and the matter of one thing (grass) becomes the matter for another (cow). If when I know what a dog is, I were to become a dog, then I would not know it for the simple reason that I would no longer be around to know it. Thus, knowing is an immaterial communion of natures: it is to be another thing in an immaterial way. Only an immaterial thing could simultaneously be more that one nature—one existentially (a human being), the other mentally (a dog or a cucumber or a computer).

If we really do possess an immaterial faculty, then it is untrue to say that all that is real is material. Materialism cannot explain all that we hold to be real, not even, as it turns out, itself. For if materialism is true, it turns out to be false. If materialism is true, then there are no universals; and if there are no universals, then there are no grounds for saying that materialism is universally true, which is precisely what the materialist wants to argue. Materialism is an indefensible position because to defend it one must use reason and explanation, and these are not themselves explainable in purely materialistic terms. In fact, pure materialism could have no terms at all, if one considers terms to be part of a language of communication. Communication involves sharing the same meaning, and what is material cannot be shared without division, that is, without the part that is parceled out differing from the original, which itself has been changed by the parceling out. Thus, if we take our thinking seriously, we may not say that all that is real is matter. Might it not be, then, that all that is real is immaterial, apprehended by the mind alone? This is the philosophical position known as idealism which we have met several times already in our discussion. It is the position espoused by Plato and Neoplatonism in the ancient tradition and taken up again in various forms by Descartes and his followers in the modern age. Such a theory, when applied to the question of what it is to be human, comes up with an argument and conclusion that looks something like this: knowledge is of the immaterial; we have knowledge; therefore, we must be immaterial. For Plato the human being is the rational soul, not the body. The soul naturally yearns to be free from the body and allowed to return to communion with the world of the Forms, those immaterial realities with which it is akin. The only problem with Plato's position is that it fails to account for the obvious fact that the soul is united to the body now. On Plato's hypothesis, it cannot be for the good of the soul, for the body hinders the soul from achieving its full perfection. Is it, then, for the good of the body? Again, this does not make any sense, on Plato's terms, for the soul is obviously better than the body, since the soul is real while the body is unreal. Plato and his followers the Neoplatonists (and all rationalists in the idealist camp) have this fundamental problem explaining the evidence that, right now, the human being is a composite of soul and body, that is, the immaterial and the material.

Aristotle, who was Plato's pupil, agrees with Plato that thinking indicates that the human being possesses an immaterial faculty. He attempts to solve the problem of why the soul and body are united by saying that the body is for the good of the soul. The rational soul makes use of the body to provide it with materials for its own function of thinking and knowing. Rather than saying, with Plato, that knowing is remembering what the disembodied soul understood when, before its incarceration in the body, it gazed on the immaterial realities which are the source of all that is real in this world, Aristotle says that the rational soul abstracts what is universal from sense experience; that is, the mind considers what something has in common with other things. For example, if we consider our old friend Spot, what the mind understands about Spot is his "dogginess" or his "spanielity" or his "aliveness," etc. Knowledge begins in the senses but transcends them. Far from the soul being chained within the body against its will, Aristotle claims that the unity of soul and body is natural and for the good of the whole human being. The human being is the composite of soul and body with the soul acting as the source of life and the structuring principle of the body. So insistent is Aristotle on the unity of soul and body, that he is willing to admit that when the body is corrupted, the human being is destroyed.

The problem for Aristotle is what to do, in the final analysis, with reason. If reason is of the immaterial, then it is the act of an immaterial faculty. But the immaterial, having no parts, cannot be divided and destroyed by any act of nature. If the individual human being is destroyed when the body corrupts, what happens to the faculty of reason which is the form of the body? To account for the fact that we do reason and that reason cannot be corrupted, Aristotle assigns reason to an outside source, which is eternal. Reason is our visitor: it is lent to us while we live and returns to its source when we die. Thus, it appears that it is not really "I" who thinks and wills but some other who thinks through me. But this raises fundamental problems. How does one explain the immediate conviction that it is "I" who knows and wills? How does one explain discovery by one person and not another, or the communication between persons? How does one explain acts of free choice that some embrace but not others? How, indeed, can the human being be a particular unity of form and matter if the form is not ultimately the form of this particular human being?

Aristotle's position has the merit of recognizing that thinking and sensing are both real activities which cannot be reduced to each other. In a sense, he tries to mediate between materialism and idealism. That one thinks cannot be explained by one's being material; that one senses cannot be explained except as one is material. But for the human mind to understand how the material and the immaterial can be at once in one being is extremely difficult, and in the end Aristotle sacrifices the evidence that it is "I" who thinks and wills in order to preserve the unity of the human being. To explain how a being that senses and thinks can be one without denying thought (with the materialists), or denying sense (with Plato and the idealists), or finally denying that it is "I" who thinks (with Aristotle)–this was the challenge which faced Aquinas.

Aquinas meets this challenge by affirming all three evidences: I *think*; I *sense*; and *I* think and sense. I have a rational soul; this soul is the form of the body; and this soul is *my* soul. All three of these statements are true, and can be known to be true by thinking about what goes on when we are thinking. First of all, we know that thinking is about what is universal and hence immaterial. Therefore, thinking is an activity which can receive the universal and immaterial, i.e., one that is not bound by particularity of matter. This component of our being we call the rational soul. Secondly, we know that thinking makes use of the raw information we receive from the senses and what the imagination supplies. We learn about the world experientially, and imagination accompanies all our thinking.[4] Thus, the rational soul is the kind of soul which requires a body to help it understand. Thirdly, it is "I" who am doing the thinking which makes use of sensation and imagination. I am not the body, but neither am I the soul. I am the unity of body and soul. They are, in a way, parts of me.

This very process we are undertaking of thinking about thinking reveals the first point–that the rational soul is immaterial. Self-awareness is possible only on the condition that the thing which possesses it can somehow stand outside itself without being different from itself. Obviously a material thing cannot do this, for it cannot be two

---

[4]For this reason good metaphors and analogies are helpful to understanding, and bad ones are disastrous.

places at once. If it tried, only part of it would be in the one place and part of it the another. Thus, an apple skin does not really surround the whole apple, because the skin itself is part of the apple. But an immaterial being, such as a human being in its rationality, can be two places at once, or two times at once, in the sense that it is not defined or confined by place and time. Through thinking about one's thinking or one's existence (which are acts of self-awareness), one does, in a way, overlap oneself. Transcending space, one stands outside oneself, reflecting on what or who one is. Transcending time, one thinks about what one did yesterday. The human being knows things and wills things and knows that it knows and wills them. I know that the apple is red, and I know that I know that the apple is red. I choose to act in a certain way, and I know that I choose to act in a certain way. It is this ability to know oneself which presents one with the ability (and responsibility) to focus one's thinking to understand a difficult idea, or to examine one's motivations in order to act in the best possible way.

As for the second point about the unity of soul and body, beyond saying that the soul requires the body to aid it in its thinking, Aquinas says that the very existence of the soul is the existence of the composite. It is not that a rational soul is tacked on to a body: this is too close to Plato's notion of the soul being in the body as a pilot is in a ship. Although the soul has an operation (thinking) which transcends the body, it is not the case that the soul exists partially separated from the body, leading, as it were, a double life. The nature of the human being is to be an embodied soul or a besouled body–however one wants to put it. The rational soul is the life of the body. There are not several souls that make up the human being, one which makes it alive (vegetative soul), one that allows it to sense (sensitive soul) and one by which it thinks (rational soul). If this were the case, then the human being would not be one thing but three things stuck together. The rational soul is the sole principle of order in the human being and so is intimately related to all aspects of the body.

This leads us to the third point: thinking is the act of the individual human being and not some universal thinker thinking through the individual. All of John's acts are particular to him, for he is a unity. His acts of sensation are obviously his own because they depend on his materiality. But his acts of thinking are just as much his own, first of all, because they too depend on his materiality insofar as the mind draws what it knows from what the senses present, but also, and more immediately evident, because both John's sensing and his thinking depend on John. As Aquinas writes: "It is the very same man himself who perceives that he understands and that he senses."[5] What Aquinas has done here is simply to take what Aristotle said seriously. Aristotle had made the fundamental claim, as against his master Plato (who insisted that the ordering principles or unchangeable Forms of things exist apart from the things), that the soul is immediately present in this human being as the life-giving and structuring principle of the body. For Aristotle the concrete material things of the world are really real. Their meaningfulness is in what they are, not in a separated Platonic world of perfect paradigms. What makes a tree a tree is not somehow outside the particular tree, but in the tree itself. Aristotle's is the common-sense position that things are really what they are, not imitations of something else. But in the end, Aristotle seems to slip back into Platonism by saying

---

[5]*Summa Theologiae* I, 76, 1.

that reason is not really the individual's, but exists in itself apart from John and Susan and Mary, one general intellect in which, for a time, we share. All Aquinas really does is to call Aristotle to remain true to his insight. Aquinas insists on the unity of soul and body, so much so that he will not allow that one's thinking is not one's own.

Thus, Aquinas uses the insight of Plato on the nature of thinking to point out the absurdity of straight materialism, uses the insight of Aristotle on the unity of soul and body to point out the absurdity of Platonic idealism, and finally deepens Aristotle's insistence on the unity of the human being to point out the absurdity in Aristotle's implied claim that reason comes to us from outside, that it is not really we who are thinking. Aquinas makes the quite commonsensical statement that we are both sensing and thinking beings, a statement which carries with it the rather astounding consequence that we are both material and immaterial. How this can be so remains mysterious, for the material and the immaterial would appear to share no common ground; but that it must be so, if we can sense and think (and this is certain), is a truth we abandon only if we are willing to fall into the absurdity of denying what we know to be true.

Let me present two short quotes from Aquinas here to underscore what we have said so far. His treatise on the human being in his *Summa Theologiæ* is prefaced and designated in the following way: "On the human being who is composed of a spiritual and a corporeal substance." We are, in a way, two things: an immaterial thing (the rational soul, and a material thing) the composite of soul and body. This goes against what Plato said about our being rational souls and what Aristotle was forced to say about our being composites which are visited by rational soul. But if, to avoid the problems with the positions of

Plato and Aristotle, Aquinas says that the human being is two substances, is he not bound to forfeit the unity of the human being? The answer is no, and it is his radical metaphysics of creation that allows him to avoid this dualistic position.

Recall from the last chapter that Aquinas distinguishes *what* things are from the fact *that* things are. In order for things to be *of certain kinds*, things must *be*–that is, they must exist. Hence, prior (in metaphysical dependence, not temporal precedence) to the principle which makes a thing be what it is (its essence), there is the principle which makes it to be at all (its existence). However, as we also said in the last chapter, this existence is the existence of the thing, not sleight-of-hand work of God. Existence is a gift and, as such, is *really* given to things. It is this principle of existence which provides the unity above the diversity we recognize in what it is to be human. Existence makes the two substances to be one. Thus Aquinas says: "The soul communicates that existence in which it subsists to the corporeal matter, out of which and the intellectual soul there is made one thing, so that the existence which is of the whole composite is also the existence of the soul."[6] The existence of the soul is the existence of the composite. Two substances are one. This is Aquinas's technical way of answering the problem. But it should be remembered that such an explanation is not the end of our consideration of the issue, for we do not know what existence is. The existence of things can be said to be a participation in God, who Aquinas says is Existence itself. But, since we do not understand what God is, we do not understand what the existence which participates in God is. We know that such a principle must be at the core of

---

[6]*Summa Theologiae* I, 76, 1 ad 5.

every thing, but we do not define it. We do not relegate it to our pool of comprehended meaning. What it is to be human remains a mystery calling us to deeper and deeper meaning. Let us now explore some of that meaning.

Three very important consequences follow from this analysis of what it is to be human. One concerns the way in which human beings come into existence, which is unique among material things. Another has to do with the way in which human beings are individuals, which again is unique among material beings. The last concerns what happens to human beings when they die. Here again we shall find that human beings present a unique case among the things of this material world.

Concerning our origin, we must first of all understand that to recognize that human beings think is to discover that they do not come to be merely through the materialistic process of change we call evolution. In understanding, the rational soul partakes of the immaterial. Since a material activity, such as sense or imagination, can discover nothing immaterial, it must be through an immaterial activity that understanding takes place. And because no material organ can register immaterial reality, the component of our being which performs this activity of knowing–the rational soul–must be immaterial. If the soul is immaterial, it obviously does not come to be from matter. What are the other options?

To begin with, there are the positions of Plato and Aristotle, which both hold that the rational soul does not come to be. The only kind of coming to be understood by the Greeks was the change of one thing into another. This kind of change, which involves the destruction of one thing as the other comes to be, always takes place in the context of materiality and time, and hence what transcends matter and time (such as the rational soul) cannot come to be in this way. For Plato, each particular human soul has always been. This is how it knows everything: it has seen it all before. For Aristotle, each individual rational soul is a temporary participation in a higher reason which has always been. But for Aquinas, the coming to be of the individual is just that: a brand new beginning of the complete person–body and soul. However, he also recognized that the soul could not be a product of change. What are the possible candidates for the origin of the soul?

They would appear to be three: the soul itself, some other immaterial thing, or God the creator. It is obvious that I did not make myself. Had I done so, I would have existed before I came to exist, which is an obvious impossibility. What about the possibility of the rational soul being made by some other greater immaterial thing, what Aquinas called a separate substance or angel? Although this could avoid the contradiction of something being and not being simultaneously, there is the fundamental problem of how an immaterial thing can be made. In the last chapter we said that, in the order of metaphysical analysis, when one reaches immaterial necessary beings, there is no accounting for their existence except by saying that there is a being which has the infinite power necessary to bring something into being from nothing (being and non-being are infinitely far apart). No created being, human or angelic, could bring something into being from nothing because every creature is, by definition, finite–that is, other than the infinite creator. And so we see that the only explanation for my being rational is that there is a creator who makes my rational soul from nothing. The coming of each human being into the world involves an act of creation. Understanding this is a direct insight into the existence of God the creator.

Here, through an examination of what it is to be human, we have come across another proof for the existence of God. The material universe cannot account for the existence of the rational soul, nor can any other created thing, since an immaterial thing can only come to be through an infinite power. Thus, the existence of the rational soul implies the existence of the creating God.

This is not, by the way, a wholesale condemnation of the theory of evolution. God is not the only cause of all that it is to be human. Aquinas would have been perfectly willing to accept the theory of evolution as a way of explaining how our bodies came to the state where they could receive a rational soul. In fact, his great master Augustine, at the end of the fourth century, had already propounded a theory of species developing through time.[7] What Aquinas would never have accepted is the idea of mind evolving from matter.

It is true that our minds require matter to help them think: whenever we think, there *is* a chemical reaction going on in the brain. But the essence of thinking–what distinguishes it from sensing or imagining–is that it knows what is universal and timeless, and what is universal and timeless must be immaterial. To the extent that something operates without matter, that thing cannot be caused by matter. To the extent that we know, we are not the products of evolution. The rational soul is created, that is, directly dependent on God and not the product of a process of material nature. In every act of knowing we have reason to affirm the existence of the creating God.

---

[7]This is Augustine's theory of God's creation of "seminal reasons" which are the seeds of things that will later develop.

This insight into the createdness of the rational soul leads us to the second important consequence of Aquinas's analysis of human nature: human beings are individuals in a unique way. Stones and other inanimate things are individuals almost entirely due to the division of matter. This piece of granite differs from that one in size and weight. There is no essential reason why they are individuals; they are all one kind of stuff that just happens to be broken into pieces. When it comes to living things such as roses and elephants, there is an essential reason for their being distinct individuals. Since living material beings do not last forever, it is necessary for the continuation of the species (or for the evolution of new species) that there be a continually renewed stream of procreative individuals. Aquinas says that the structure of the universe in its unity and the interconnectedness of its parts demands that there be some continuity of kinds and this is only accomplished among living things through the continued procreation by individuals within the species.

When we consider human beings, the first two explanations of individuality apply, but there is a third and overriding reason why human beings are individuals. Not only does each human individual inhabit a different body, and as a procreating individual serve to preserve the species, but each human being is an individual for his or her own sake. We do belong to a species of animals, but our place in the order of things is not reducible to that. Each human individual, as rational, is a permanent, essential feature of the universe. Our rationality cannot be reduced to nature and the structure of the material world. Each rational being transcends the material universe and is fundamental to the order of the whole creation. Each is a unique center of conscious life.

The importance of the individual human being is made even clearer by saying, as Aquinas does, that each is, in a way, all things. Each human being has the potentiality to recreate the world through knowing it. Although at any given time one's knowledge is finite, there is no intrinsic limit to what one can know about the universe. Aquinas says that the human being is the matrix of the universe, the only being which is both material and immaterial. The individual human being is not ordained to a further, more important, purpose within the universe, as individuals of other species are ordained for the preservation of the species; rather, the purpose of the universe appears, surprisingly, to be the production of individual human beings. The universe with its necessary guiding forces and its evolution can be seen as existing for the sake of human beings. The material process of evolution has led to the complexity of the human body which is fitting material for thought to inhabit. Matter has evolved to the point where it can, in a sense, justify its evolution—to the point where (by being part of the unity which is the human being) it can know itself. Of course, one does not attribute the intentionality of this process to matter as a blind unfolding of chance events, but to the prior order of the guiding laws of the universe and ultimately to the intelligent creator of that ordered universe.

Each individual human being is thus a new creation, both in the sense that each, as having a rational soul, must be created directly by God, and in the further sense that each recreates the world. Each individual takes his or her place in the order of the universe, a permanent addition to the structure and meaning of all things. Human beings are not reducible to members of the species. For this reason, all kinds of arguments for policies which would sacrifice individuals for the good of the whole, or weed out unwanted elements to create a master race, or eliminate the elderly or the unborn to make a better world for the majority are fundamentally flawed. Each individual matters and is irreducible to the material world, or to the human species, or even to the universe as a whole.

If human beings are permanent features of the universe, what is the nature of that permanent state? It is on the issue of what happens after death that Aquinas's analysis of what it is to be human yields its third fruitful consequence of meaning. Of course, we do not have the advantage of directly experiencing what is to be our state after death, but certain things follow from what we hold ourselves to be right now. It is a question that reaches into mystery, but not chaos, for what we know human nature to be now provides us with windows on what happens after death. Lest we think of this as a merely religious question, we need only point out that pagan Greek philosophers of many persuasions raised it. It is a human question, one we raise naturally because, unlike other living things in this world, we know that we shall die.

There are two standard philosophical answers to what happens after death–one materialist and one idealist. The materialists answer that, since all that is real is the material composition of the human being, the dissolution of that composition which is death is the end of the individual. Either there is an absolute end of everything as the atomists and the Epicureans held, or, for a pantheism like Stoicism, one returns to the whole material universe and continues to be a part of the cosmic life. In either case, the individual ceases to exist. Idealists like Plato would answer that death frees the soul (which is the individual) from the "death" that is communion with the body. Physical death is a return to the natural state of the soul, one free of the body. Here indeed there is an individual immortality, but at the cost of denying that having a body is essential to being human.

As we have said before, Aquinas disagrees with both positions. He points out to the materialists that thinking cannot be explained by matter, and that therefore we have an element that cannot be corrupted. With Plato, Aquinas says that the rational soul must live on. But against Plato, and with Aristotle, Aquinas insists that the human being is the composite of soul and body. Thinking and sensing are both the operations of the human being. The human soul is naturally united to the body, and this union is not contrary to the good of the soul, but for its good. Does this leave us with Aristotle's option? Must we say that since reason transcends the body, and since the individual is the composite of soul and body, at death the individual is destroyed and reason returns to some transcendent power from which it was temporarily and inexplicably borrowed?

Aquinas answers no. There is another option, one as absolutely foreign to the Greek philosophical tradition as creation–it is the resurrection of the body. Like the doctrine of creation, the idea that the body will be resurrected after death had a religious origin. Among the Jews, in the centuries before the beginning of the Christian era, the Pharisees interpreted the Scriptures as pointing to the resurrection of the body, while the Sadducees did not. The doctrine is confirmed by the teaching of Christ. However, in the same way that he holds creation to be a philosophical as well as a theological truth, Aquinas argues that the resurrection of the body is reasonable and not merely a matter of faith. As we pointed out earlier, the existence of the rational soul is the very existence of the composite. The unity of the human being is so strong that the immortality of the rational soul is the immortality of the body. Such a conclusion is, at the very least, surprising. Let us take some time to look at the pieces of Aquinas's argument. What are the truths in tension that Aquinas holds steadily before his gaze, and how are they related?

To start with, Aquinas insists that the rational soul must be immortal. He rejects materialism for its meaningless-ness. As we have said repeatedly, the rational soul is im-mortal because it has an activity of its own which does not involve the body. This conclusion can be denied only by saying, with the materialists, that we do not really think. For if thinking is a matter of matter, then it doesn't matter–all is meaningless. If materialism is true, all arguments–including the one for its own justification–fail. If any arguments are valid, if anything is true, then mate-rialism is false and we have an immaterial rational nature which is immortal.

In addition to claiming that rationality means immortal-ity, Aquinas insists that rationality is individual, and so the individual rational soul is immortal. The evidence for at-tributing immortality to the *individual* rational soul is the evidence of my thinking and willing. What sense can it make to attribute activities that are immediately recog-nized as mine to someone else? Communication and freedom are realities only if my thinking and choosing are my own. Aristotle gives up the possibility of individual immortality in the name of the unity of body and soul. For if the individual soul were immortal, then what would one call it? Would it be the human being? Aristotle does not want to say this because it would deny that to be a body is to be human. Now Aquinas is in full agreement with Aristotle on this point, but he will not give up the obvious truth that thinking is the act of the individual merely because the unity of the composite human being appears to be threatened by allowing that an individual rational soul can live on without the body.

Pushing further into this very problem of unity, Aquinas finds, not that our materiality makes individual immortality impossible, but rather (and this his unique contribution to the discussion) that the immortality of the rational soul, in the final analysis, depends on the unity of soul and body, and that this unity demands that the body be resurrected. Plato's position could allow for individual immortality, but only by rejecting our materiality. In Plato's idealism, each soul has always existed and is repeatedly reincarnated until by the practice of philosophy it transcends the material world to dwell forever in the immaterial reality of the Forms. Aristotle, to save our materiality, rejects individual immortality. Aquinas holds both that we are individually immortal and that we are material, and that these two positions are not mutually exclusive but belong together and complete each other. This surprising conjunction of seemingly contradictory ideas deserves some more attention.

Aquinas says, with Aristotle, that the human soul is not the human being, but part of the human being. The rational soul is naturally the life of the body. It is the kind of soul that requires a body to be what it is; or better, to avoid sounding like the soul exists prior to the body, let us say that the *human being* requires a rational soul as the life-giving and structuring principle of a body. Here we have the two substances–Plato's rational soul and Aristotle's composite–in unity. The rational soul is created by God to give life to and structure the biological being which is the product of parents, evolution, and the laws of the universe. The rational soul–that part of the human being which cannot be a product of material nature–is created to be one with that product of material nature. The nature of the rational soul is to be one with the body.

Because the soul has a life of its own in the sense that it operates on one level without the body, one might think that its relation to the body is tenuous. The relationship between horse and cart is tenuous in this way. Since the horse may operate without the cart, galloping over the fields, it is clear that it does not belong naturally with the cart. But for the soul's relationship with the body, this is anything but true. Unlike horse and cart, which no one would claim to be one thing, Aquinas is saying that the rational soul and the body are one, and for verification he appeals to one's reflection on what it is to be human. The relation between the soul and the matter it structures (the body) is unique among the things we know. As the principle of order for the human being, the soul's bond with what it unifies and enlivens is stronger that of any other thing. The structuring and life-giving form of lamb is destroyed by the structuring and life-giving form of lion. Tomato plants are destroyed by cutworms. Iron is destroyed by water. Even the smallest particles of physics may be destructible, for, after all, the atom (literally, the "unsplittable") has been split. But the rational soul cannot be destroyed since it is immaterial. Therefore, its natural relation to a particular body can never fail to exist. The desire of the rational soul to give life to a particular body is permanent.

Since the rational soul is naturally the life of the body, the separation of soul and body which we witness as death is unnatural. Since death is "the way of all things" (apparently, the most natural of occurrences), let us pause to reflect on what is unnatural about death. It is true enough that dissolution and death are natural to a material being, for to be material is to be in continuity with other material things and, therefore, to be able to change into something else. A material thing is actually one particular kind of thing, but it can become something else. Water can become oxygen and hydrogen; grass can become cow; the material of one human being can become hydrogen, grass, cow, or even part of another human being. What is composed of a diversity of unlike elements, such as the human being, tends towards dissolution. This is just the principle of entropy (things tend to disorder) that modern science recognizes as universally true for the material universe. However, although natural for the material composite to decay, it is unnatural for the rational soul to be separated from the composite, for the rational soul is created as the life-giving structuring principle of the human being. Since the existence and life of the composite depends on the existence of the rational soul and not vice versa, it is appropriate to say that it is unnatural for the soul and body to be separated. The separation goes against the permanent, natural inclination within the soul to be the life of this body. But the unnatural cannot last forever. Throw a stone up; it comes back down. Plunge a burning branch into water; it is soon extinguished. It is unnatural for the stone to move away from the center of gravity, and it is unnatural for fire to burn under water. Likewise, it is unnatural for the soul to be separated from the body, and so this separation cannot last forever. Therefore, there will be a resurrection of the body.

Another way of putting this is to say that the rational soul has a natural desire for the body and that such a natural desire cannot be in vain. The rational soul is not made separately and then for some reason associated with the body for a time: it is made to be with the body. If the soul were to be separated from the body, it would naturally desire reunification. And this natural desire could never cease since the soul is permanent. Because a natural desire cannot be in vain, there will be a reunification, and this reunification is known as the resurrection of the body.

Why is it that a natural desire cannot be in vain? To be in vain means to be to no purpose. But what is natural is precisely what has purpose; what is natural to a thing is something without which that thing could not be what it is. It is what a thing is essentially all about. To lose a natural desire is for a thing to cease to be. If a natural desire is not fulfilled, then a nature is not fulfilled. Now for nonrational being, the natural desire need not be fulfilled by any particular individual, for the individual has a purpose beyond it, the continuation of the species. But the individual human being is its own purpose, an essential part of the universe; therefore, for the human being's desire for embodiment to go unfulfilled is for a natural desire to go permanently unfulfilled, for human nature to fail to be what it is. For a permanent being whose essence requires the unity of body and soul to be permanently without part of its essence (the body) is for something *to be* and *not be* at the same time—a contradiction. Therefore, there must be a resurrection: it is demanded by what we presently know a human being to be.

Now I think it finally can be understood why Aquinas thinks that the immortality of the soul depends on the unity of body and soul. If we reject the resurrection of the body, that is, if we reject the naturalness of our being embodied reason, then it is clear that we shall have a hard time proving that the soul is immortal. For if the soul is naturally the form of the body, then to say that it can naturally exist on a permanent basis apart from the body is to be in contradiction. If the rational soul is immortal apart from the body, then it is not a *human* rational soul, for the human rational soul is the life of a particular body. Thus Aquinas writes: "If the resurrection of the body is denied, it is not easy but difficult to uphold the immortality of the soul."[8]

But how can the resurrection happen when the body remains where we can see it, but without its principle of life? This flesh and these bones are quite apparently left behind. They decay and their basic parts become parts of other things and even other human beings. How then can there be a particular resurrected body, the same as the one with which the soul was united in this life? Aquinas's answer is to say that my body is not essentially these particular atoms which I possess now or at my death. It is obvious, upon reflection, that I have had the same body (never someone else's) all my life; but we know that the body is constantly replenishing itself with new material. The food comes in; some of it stays and becomes me. Thus, the body is not a particular batch of atoms, but a structure. But what is the source of this structure? If the human being is one thing, then there is only one principle of unity, and that principle accounts for all aspects of being human. The unifying and structuring principle of the human being is the rational soul. There is not a bodily structure joined to a mental structure, or the human being would be two things extrinsically joined together, with no internal principle of unity. This scenario is contrary to the unified person one knows oneself to be. Aquinas's conclusion is that the essential structure or pattern or meaning of the body is contained in the rational soul, and so that pattern which is me is not lost when this particular expression of my body is left behind at death.

---

[8] *I ad Corinthios*, 15, L. 2.

But what about the problem of continuity? We have spoken of separation and being left behind. If the soul and body really are separated, what sense can there be in suggesting that the resurrected unity will be identical with the one we recognize in this life? It seems there will have to be a break in time when the soul is without the body, that is, when the individual human being has ceased to be. In answer to this problem, one may say simply that to speak of a break in time is to speak inappropriately about the soul's state of separation from the body. There is no break in time for the soul itself, since, as immaterial, it does not exist in time. Continuity is a temporal term, and therefore applicable only to what is material. Therefore, the issue of a break in continuity, of a time when the soul is separated from the body, is not to the point. Although this explanation may not dispel all questions about the transition, it does at least deny that continuity in time is an issue. The soul provides the identity for the transition, and the soul in itself is not in time.

However, in order to answer the question of how a body may be provided for the soul once it has lost its relationship with the matter of this world, we must look for a cause outside the soul. Although the continuity between this unified life of soul and body and the resurrected life can be provided by the soul, how can the rational soul be resupplied with its own particular body? The material universe, which provided the original matter through the process of evolution and human sexual intercourse, cannot do it, for material nature operates in ways peculiar to a time and place and therefore cannot generate the same material thing twice. Nor can the rational soul provide itself with the particular matter required for a body. Finite being can make something only out of pre-existing matter. Therefore, the rational soul, as a created and hence finite being, is restricted by the qualifications of material coming to be which we just specified. The only other option for making is creation. But no finite thing can create, since an infinite power is required to bring something from non-being to being. For this reason, Aquinas insists that the resurrection will also require the activity of God the creator.

In this way the resurrection of the body is miraculous, but its being miraculous does not make it unnatural. We saw in the second chapter that the world is created. Its being created, however, does not make it unnatural. We saw earlier in this chapter that the coming to be of every human being requires the direct hand of God the creator, but we do not on that account say that the coming to be of a child is unnatural. Similarly, to say that the resurrection of the body requires God's creating hand is not to deny its being in some way natural.

We are left with one obvious question which has not as yet been addressed: why is it that the soul and body are ever separated if such a separation is unnatural? Unnatural things do, of course, happen: a stone may be thrown up against its natural inclination to join the center of the earth; trees are cut and formed to build houses; plants and animals are genetically engineered to serve humanity. In all these cases it is because something outside the nature of the particular thing intervenes that the activity may be said to be unnatural. What is it that intervenes in human nature which makes the separation of rational soul and body possible? There is no natural answer to this question: here we are face to face with mystery. Why stones go up and trees become houses and new species of plants are produced by genetic engineering can be answered by pointing to another natural force within the universe –human beings. But there appears to be no natural

answer to why the rational soul and body must separate.
If the form and structure of the human being is contained
in the rational soul, and if the rational soul is immaterial
and therefore unable to be altered by material forces
within the universe, then nothing in the universe external
to the human being can be the cause of this separation.

The only answer which Aquinas offers to this particular
question is theological–which is not to say without meaning, but without a perfectly clear natural explanation. The
reason why soul and body separate is sin. Sin, as we shall
see in Chapter Five, is not a natural element in the world,
but a defect in human nature. It is not some external in-
tervention upon our nature, but an internal failure. It is
the failure to be reasonable in our choices; it is the failure
to be human. We sinned (and sin–which is to act against
our nature as reasonable creatures) and so lost the integ-
rity of the rational soul. With its loss of reason, the rational soul lost its ability to give life to the composite, both
as to the life of reason and as to biological life. There is no
trouble with the facts, here. We do sin; and we do die.
Sin is unnatural, for it is a failure to live up to our nature
as reasonable beings; and it appears to be unnatural for
the rational soul, which is by nature one with the body, to
be separated from that body.

The connection between the two is not one of natural
demonstration, for there is a move from the order of moral
failure to the order of metaphysical failure; but neither is
the connection unreasonable, for one failure may occasion
another. Here is fruitful ground for meditation.

Why human beings originally sinned (and why we sin)
is mysterious, because it requires a choice of reason and
yet is always against reason. As sin is mysterious, so is it
mysterious (although obviously true) that the immortal
soul which is naturally the form of the body should not

always possess unity with the body—that is, that human beings die. Through failing, by sinning, to abide by our natural desire to be reasonable, we failed to achieve our desire for immortal unity with the body. God's grace is required to restore that unity in the resurrection. However, God's grace is not the enemy and destroyer of nature, but its ally and perfecter. Nature favors the unity of rational soul and body; and thus it favors the resurrection, since the soul is the life-giving principle of the composite, and the soul is immortal.

Since material things naturally decay, when we think of ourselves as material, we think of ourselves as decaying; but death is an accidental, not an essential, condition of being human. We know the essence or nature of something by knowing its form, in which the whole intelligibility of the thing is present. When we talk about the "form" of something, we are talking about what can be known about it, what is intrinsically meaningful about that thing. The form of the human being is the rational soul. Therefore, we take what is natural to the human being from the soul, not the body. In the words of Aquinas: "It is clear that the existence of matter and form is one, for matter does not have actual existence unless by form."[9] The fact that the rational soul is the form of the body tells us that the unity of body and soul is natural and that the separation at death is unnatural, and it tells us that the resurrection is required for the completion of our nature, even while it is possible only with the help of God.

---

[9]*Summa contra Gentiles* IV, 81, [11]. The terms "form" and "matter" are used by Aristotle and Aquinas to explain two aspects of material things. "Form" indicates what something is; it is its intrinsic structuring principle. "Matter" indicates that the thing can change into something else.

There is one more common objection which is raised against the truth of the resurrection of the body. Strangely enough, this objection may be raised by either believers or nonbelievers. Put briefly, the objection runs as follows: the resurrection of the body is purely a matter of faith and is a gift granted to believers as a reward for being good. A believer might argue that, since we are all sinners, we cannot count on the resurrection of the body. It is our faith and our hope. A nonbeliever might prefer to call it mere wish-fulfillment. Both might agree in saying that somehow the resurrection of the body has nothing to do with nature. Both, I think, are mistaken.

It is true that the resurrection of the body is part of the creed, but it is not true that the faith holds that the resurrection of the body is given to the good as a reward. All will be resurrected, the good and the bad. The good will be resurrected to eternal Life; the bad resurrected to eternal Death. The everlasting life of which we have spoken in this chapter is quite as compatible with spiritual Death as with spiritual Life. Understood in this way, the doctrine of the resurrection, with its insistence on the continuance of conscious bodily existence either of happiness or of misery, far from being wish-fulfillment, is rather a sobering reminder of our permanent responsibility for our acts. There is, of course, the possibility of forgiveness, but there is no escape through annihilation.

Understanding the resurrection of the body as the third important consequence of Aquinas's position on what it is to be human has lead us to the threshold of mystery, which is to say, to the very cutting edge of meaning, where our minds stretch to understand what cannot be completely comprehended. Once more we are confronted with the activity of God which, though it cannot be explained by nature, is seen to be, not an alternative and thus a destroyer of nature, but rather the guarantee and fulfillment of nature. In fact, what we know about the natural requirement for the resurrection is yet one more way of underscoring the insight that God the creator exists. For if the rational soul is immortal and the form of the body, and its reunion with the body is a requirement of its nature, but the soul cannot provide itself with a resurrected body (nor can any finite thing), then there must be a creator to grant this resurrected body to the soul.

What we can say about human nature, we should say: as an explanation of the ultimate state of the human being, the resurrection of the body is a more reasonable position, more faithful to what it is to be human, than that of the materialists or Plato or Aristotle. Therefore, we should accept it as the most philosophically respectable position. The fact that the human being requires the activity of God to fulfill its natural end should not make us reject the resurrection of the body; for, as we discovered in Chapter Two, God's presence to things does not dissolve their naturalness, but creates it.

We have had rather a long meditation on what human nature implies for our ultimate end. Let now us review what we have said are the evidences reason gathers when puzzling out what it is to be human. When we consider the nature of the human being, we discover two truths in apparent conflict. There is obvious evidence that what we are is material: we see, feel, hear, and stub our toes up against the world. There is also obvious evidence that what we are is immaterial: the very idea that we are either material or immaterial is the fruit of an activity that goes beyond the material–the activity we call reason. If we say that we are merely material, then we cannot account for our saying so, nor defend our statement. In a different but equally important way, if we say that we are merely soul, we cannot account for our saying so. Language is central to being human, and while it involves an immaterial component in the thought it expresses, it also requires a material component in the body, vocal chords, hands, etc., required to express the thought.

Not only are both of these two apparently conflicting truths confirmed by natural evidence, but they actually turn out to be mutually supportive and together guarantee the unity of the individual human being. Like the opposite poles of a magnet, the opposition of these truths does not repel, but attracts, binding fast the various aspects of our being human into an indissoluble unity of mind and matter. To say we have an ordering principle of life (the rational soul) which transcends the material in its operation is not to fragment the unity of the human being, but to guarantee it. It is precisely because the rational soul is immaterial that it can never lose its essential characteristic, which is to be the life and structuring principle of a particular body. Nothing in the universe can make it change: it remains permanently the life of a particular body. Thus, having a soul which transcends the body makes me more certainly me, body and soul. On the other hand, so far is the body from denying the immortal life of the soul, that the soul without the body cannot be the immortal thing that its operation claims it is. For if the soul is the life of the body, and this is what we know it to be right now, then to say that it can live forever without the body is to be involved in denying the natural–that is, denying what natural reason tells us about what we are. It is to say that a permanent nature can be permanently what it is not, which is a contradiction. Thus, the soul's relation to the body is good for the body, and the body's relation to the soul is good for the soul. Each is a guarantee of the other's well-being.

Let us recall, as we close this chapter, that everything we have said about the nature of the human being–its origin, its individuality, and its end–is taken from what we know now about what it means to be human. Reason, indeed, has opened up a world of new questions, a world of wonder. It has led us to the edge of mystery, to the frontier where meaning extends beyond our complete comprehension. Some of the conclusions we have reached stretch beyond what is contained in the natural universe of things. But this is not because we have smuggled the supernatural into the evidence. Rather, we have seen that the supernatural (the activity of God the creator) is required in order that the natural may be what it is. In order that a human being may be born, there is required the direct creative activity of God, for nothing in the universe can make an immaterial thing such as the rational soul. Then again, it is because of this created rational soul with its universal scope of understanding that human beings are unique individuals, permanent features of the universe, not grist for the mill of scientific experiment or social planning. Finally, in order that the human being may not cease to be what it is naturally–an indestructible rational soul giving life to a body–there will be a resurrection of the body, with God recreating (or creating, for it comes to the same thing) the new matter of the resurrected human being. If one would be faithful to reason, one is going to have to bump up against the source of reason and of all things–the creating God. This is not a defect of reason, but its natural glory.

IV
God and Human Freedom

Chapter Two focused on our asking "Why?" about things, and we discovered that the ultimate answer to this question is God the creator. Chapter Three focused on who it is who asks such a question, and we discovered that it is a thinking material being–the immortal and embodied individual. Let us now consider a couple of ways in which God and human being interact. In this chapter the topic will be the relationship between divine providence and human freedom; in the next, we shall take up the relation between God and morality. Each of these issues is especially important for how we live our lives. If the absolute certainty of God's providence makes human freedom impossible, then the whole project of social and political responsibility is a sham. For if we have no freedom, then we cannot help how we act. If, however, we see our way through this problem, and say that despite divine providence there is human freedom and hence responsibility, we run into the question of who or what dictates and constitutes this responsibility. Who says we should be moral? And in what does moral perfection lie? Does the command to be good come from God, and does our happiness lie in God alone and not in the things of this world? If the answer to these questions is yes, then what obligation is there for those who do not believe in God, and can a believer justify his actions in the name of God even if they appear to go against common morality? These issues are very important, and Aquinas has some very important things to say about them.

Let us begin by spelling out in more detail the problem that exists in claiming that God is provident and human beings are free. Recall what we have said about God. God, we said, is the reason why there is anything at all. We have a question which is not adequately answered by all the kinds of causality we can discover within the universe. The question is a very simple one, which can be raised by contact with any particular thing in our world. Knowing that we are not responsible for its existence, we ask: "Why is this thing?" Implied in this "Why?" is a question about the whole universe: "Why is there anything at all and not nothing?" The answer to this question, which must exist if there is anything (and there is), is God. God is the creating cause of all that is. As maker of everything, he must know everything which he makes, which is everything that is, was, and will be.

The problem, then, is this: if God knows everything that is and will be, and he is absolutely the first cause (hence all-powerful), then everything happens according to what God knows and wills. This conclusion does not bother us much, I think, when applied to things which perform their activities with no awareness at all or with the automatic awareness provided by instinct. We do not expect these things to escape the bounds imposed on them by nature, and therefore it is not difficult to accept that these bounds are ultimately imposed by the author of nature. But when we come to apply this conclusion to ourselves as thoughtful and freely-acting individuals, we are no where near as ready to accept it. If God knows what we shall do before we do it and is the cause of our doing it, how in the world can our choices be free? Conversely, if we freely choose what we are going to do, then how in the world can God know and cause our actions? The answer, as we shall see, is that there is no way *in the world* that these two things can happen simultaneously: it is precisely because God is not in this world, but the cause of the world, that there is no contradiction.

There are three obvious moves one can make to try to avoid the problem. First of all, if one has a strong conviction of divine guidance in human activities, one will try denying free will. This was the basic position of the Greeks up to around the time of Plato and Aristotle. The world and human lives are ruled by fate. Everything happens in a predetermined way. A similar position was also held by the Protestant Reformers in their doctrine of predestination. The focus was more theological than philosophical, but the thought was the same. Luther argued that our wills are enslaved by God and that we have no choice as to whether we shall be saved or not, and Calvin sharpened this notion of predestination. Consistent materialists, ancient and modern, are obliged to take this view, for free will requires that the person exercising the free will not be completely determined by the material environment. If all that is real is material, then determinism must be the rule.

One may object that in some modern circles, the activity of matter at its most fundamental level where it is close to, if not the same as, energy, is said to be random. I do not know whether proponents of this view mean that we cannot know how the matter in its activity conforms to determined rules (which I think must be the case) or whether they mean that the matter does not conform to determined rules. The trouble with the second position is that, if we cannot know the position and velocity of a sub-atomic particle simultaneously (Heisenberg's uncertainty principle), how could we know that matter is not conform-ing? In any case, randomness is just as destructive as determinism of the freedom we mean when we talk of free choice. For a random action, like swatting a fly, is nothing like a free action, such as deciding to steal some-thing for one's own benefit or, on the other side, choosing to sacrifice what one needs for another. The random action bears no moral dimension.

The reason Plato and Aristotle withdrew from this tradi-tion of fatalism was because of an interest in ethics. This is not to say that ethical questions were not entertained in Homer, or Aeschylus or Sophocles: of course they were. But in the end, fate rules. The ancients were unable to allow systematically for the freedom that they must have assumed if they took ethical decisions seriously. If there is such a thing as moral obligation, then we must not say that all is ruled by fate. Some measure of human freedom must be allowed.

If one has a strong conviction that we have free will, there is another obvious move one can make to avoid the dilemma, and that is to deny providence. This is the posi-tion characteristic of Plato and Aristotle. Plato's Forms (which are the real models for this fleeting world) did not make the world, nor are they concerned with what goes on here. Just as the soul, which is akin to the Forms, does not naturally want to have anything to do with the imper-fections of a material world, so neither do the other Forms concern themselves with this halfway house of becoming:

what truly is (the world of the Forms) would not truly be if it descended to interact with the changing and unreal material world in which we find ourselves. Neither is Aristotle's God a provident God: he does not know what is going on in this world, nor care to know. Aristotle's God is self-thinking thought, the highest activity involved in contemplating the highest object–itself. If such a God were to think about the world, it would not be involved in contemplating the highest of all objects, and hence would cease to be God. We must remember that neither Plato nor Aristotle nor, for that matter, any pagan Greek philosopher or theologian held that God freely created the world from nothing. Not having created the world freely, God would not be responsible for there being a world, nor would he care whether there is a material world. A materialist of any time would also have to deny providence since providence is the rule of an intelligent and hence immaterial being over this world, and the materialist rejects the possibility of there being anything immaterial.

Thus, the third obvious move is that of the materialist who, if he is consistent, must deny both freedom and providence. If, because all is material, there can be no such thing as free will, and if, because all is material, there can be no one ordering the matter, then there can be no conflict between two truths, for both theses are false. If one holds a materialist metaphysics (all that is real is matter), then one can assent to there being freedom or providence only by contradicting one's metaphysics. The Stoics, for example, are famous for saying that one should hold onto one's dignity despite what goes on in the world; but if materialism is true, then the only reason one holds onto one's dignity is because one is determined to do so, that is, because one cannot avoid doing so. The exhortation to keep one's dignity cannot really be an appeal to free will if nothing in the human being transcends the material. Or, if one is a materialist, yet professes belief in providence, as did some of the philosophers of the Renaissance and Enlightenment, then one does so as a fideist, not as a philosopher. Assent to providence, in such a case, is an act of blind faith and not of reason.

These are the three obvious ways to avoid the apparent contradiction that God is provident, yet human beings are free. The only trouble with these three positions is that they reject what is obvious. There are good reasons to hold that God rules all things and good reasons to hold that human beings act freely. Therefore, to deny either or both is to go against reason. Even if one cannot understand how both can simultaneously be true of the same act, it is absurd, given the evidence that one does understand, to deny either. Thomas Aquinas takes this fourth most obvious (in the sense of following the evidence at hand) position and shows how providence and freedom are not only compatible but mutually affirming. To prepare the way for understanding how Aquinas reconciles these two points, let us look at each in some greater detail.

First, let us consider providence. In order for God to be provident, he must be the cause of all things, know all things, and be all-powerful, applying his knowledge to things in such a way that none escapes his government. Now God is absolutely simple, for if he were composite in any way, there would have to be a cause of his composition which would be prior to him. But since God is the first cause of everything, he cannot be composed in any way. Thus, if it can be shown that there is knowledge and power in God, then these will be identical and the same as his causality–that is, they will apply to all things.

There are two ways to show that God must have knowledge. One is related to the arguments of Chapter Two, and the other to the arguments of Chapter Three. The procedure we traced in pursuit of the answer to the question "Why?" was one of discovering deeper and deeper causes of the order in the world. From the immediate level of a common sense distinction between things (dog from elephant), the question deepened and the answer to it became more and more universal, including explanations from the point of view of biology, chemistry, and physics. Finally, to answer the question of why there are four great universal forces which explain all the order of the material world, we came to the answer: "because there is a world and not nothing," which is to say, because there is a creator of the ordered universe of things. Now order requires an orderer. To say that the universe is ordered because of chance is merely to throw up one's hands and say that there is not *really* any order in the universe, for chance is the opposite of order. If there is an orderer, he must have knowledge. The rule of energy in the universe is entropy which is the tendency to dissipate and fall away from order. The only example we have of anything acting against this rule is what comes from human thought and action.[1] Hence, if the universe is ordered, it comes to be so through an agent who possesses an ability to order, which is what we mean be reason. Now, of course, we have no direct insight into the knowledge and action of God and so cannot say what God's knowledge and action are in themselves. But we can know that they must account for everything in the world, and that includes the order of

---

[1]Actually, this is not quite true: the theory of evolution presents us with evidence that life itself, in its thrust toward more perfect forms, moves against this tendency of material things and energy toward decay. But then, of course, this process described by evolution is itself evidence of a principle of order which is not to be found in the natural characteristics of a material world.

things. Hence, God must be capable of making order, and this requires something like reason as we know it.

There is a shorter way to say the same thing, based on the argument for the existence of God which we met in Chapter Three. We know God exists as creator because the human mind exists, and nothing in nature can explain the mind's existence. Now common sense tells us that there cannot be more in the effect than in the cause. You cannot get ten apples from a tree that only bears nine; you cannot get a temperature of 80 degrees Fahrenheit from a radiator at 70 degrees Fahrenheit. In short, you cannot get more from less. If, therefore, there is a created being that has knowledge, then there must be knowledge in the creator. The creator's knowledge need not be just like the creature's knowledge; in fact, it cannot be, since God's is perfectly complete and simple, while ours is limited and grows through a process of learning. However we want to try to describe divine knowing, it cannot be less complete or perfect than human knowing. If it were, more would come from less, which is impossible.

God is also all-powerful. If God makes all things, he makes them as kinds of things that naturally operate in various ways. The maker of nature is also the maker of all natural activities. Therefore, the power to be and do anything is possessed in a transcendent way by the one who creates everything. Or one can look at it from the negative side. If God were not all-powerful, what would it mean? It would mean that there is something which escapes God's power, which is not created by God. In such a case what we were calling "God," which was limited in power, would not in fact be God; for God is the answer to the last question, and if he were in some way subject to some other power, the question "why?" would extend beyond him, and hence he would not be God, the creator of all things.

As we said above, the creating God is absolutely simple. If he were composed, there would have to be a cause of the composition, and so God would not be the first cause. Since God is perfectly simple, for him to create and for him to know are not two different activities, but the same thing. Thus, God's knowledge of his creation must be perfect, and it is not dependent upon his creation. This is hard for us to understand, for human knowledge depends in an essential way on the thing that is known. To know that orangutans are not baboons, one must have experience of orangutans and baboons or have learned the difference between them from someone who did have the experience. Orangutans and baboons are the measures of such knowledge. To know that you are reading a book on the thought of Aquinas, it is necessary that the book be there for you to read. The truth or falsity of our knowledge is measured by the things we know. As so clearly pointed out by Aristotle, to speak the truth is to say of what is, that it is, and of what is not, that it is not. With God it is the exact opposite. His knowledge is in no way measured by things, but rather is their measure. God's knowledge makes things be what they are. The world does not act on God: it is all one-way traffic. If the world could act on God, then God would not be first cause absolutely–that is, would not be God.

You might, at this conclusion, feel a little frustrated and slighted not to be able to affect God and might feel that God, since he is so good, could not create such an unfair situation. Or perhaps you think that if this is the kind of God that is meant, one whom you cannot affect, then you do not want such a God. But before you close your mind to such a God (and close this book), let me ask you to follow the argument a bit further; for I think you will find that only such a God can guarantee the precious things we rightly treasure, things like the very freedom that appears to be threatened by what we are saying right now about God's relationship to the world.

Before shifting to the issue of how we know we are free and how a creating God guarantees this freedom, let us make sure that we know what we are saying about God's providence. God's knowledge and power, and hence his providence, extend to absolutely everything and every activity. This means that God knows and causes my free acts, as well as the instincts of the moose, the growth of a flower, the movement of the spheres and the structure of the atom. There is nothing that escapes God's knowledge or causality. God makes everything to be the kind of thing it is whether directly, as in the case of human minds or the fundamental forces of nature, or indirectly, as in the case of stones, plants, and animals which come to be under the fundamental forces of nature. He is the creating and conserving cause of all things. But God does not act merely to keep things in being, leaving their proper activities to themselves. No, every activity, as something real, is caused by God. As Aquinas himself writes: "Just as God not only gave existence being to things when they first began to exist, but is also the cause of existence in them for as long as they exist, conserving things in existence, so also did he not only give operative powers to them when they were first made, but he always causes these powers in things. Hence, were the divine influence to cease, every operation would cease."[2] God the creator is not the clock maker God of the Enlightenment. He does not wind the world up at one moment and then let it go

---

[2]*Summa Contra Gentiles* III, 67, [3].

on its own power, indifferent to what happens in it. God is creator, conserver, and mover of all things.

But this does not take away the natures of things, including my nature to be free. For God is the cause of nature, not its undoing. We know God to exist as the cause of nature from a study of nature. Thus, in reaching the knowledge of God as creator, we do not abandon our knowledge of the things of nature. They are the foundations of knowing God; if their natures are destroyed, so is our knowledge that God is creator. Therefore, we must study the things of this world to find out what their natures are. In this case, we must consider what it is to be human if we are to know whether or not we are free. We do not consult the nature of God, simply because we do not and cannot know what God's nature is.

Thomas Aquinas's basic response to the question of whether or not we have freedom is to say that our freedom is too obvious to doubt. We do choose freely; therefore, we are free to choose. Freedom is a first principle of what Aquinas calls our practical reason. Practical reason is our way of thinking about what is good or bad, what we desire or wish to avoid; it involves the activities of recognizing options, deliberating, and choosing what we shall do. Aquinas distinguishes practical reason from theoretical reason, which is our way of thinking about what is real or unreal, what is true or false; theoretical reason involves such activities as logic, mathematics, and the hard sciences. Practical reason is about what we do and what we know to be good; theoretical reason is about what we understand and what we know to be true.

Now while it is prerequisite for freedom of choice that we be able to understand and reason theoretically (for it is the act of theoretical reason to distinguish between things, which is prerequisite for choosing between them), it does not seem to be necessary that the ability to understand and to reason theoretically be accompanied by freedom; at least this cannot be proven by theoretical reason to be so. It is possible that all our choices and acts are determined, even those which we think are free. Of course, it is also possible that our choices and acts are free. Only on the assumption that all that is real is material, and therefore subject to the necessary laws of matter in motion, can there be said to be a theoretical case for determinism. But then materialism, as you will recall, cannot justify itself. In the first place, if there are any immaterial realities, it is obvious that materialist methodology will fail to verify their existence. And secondly, if the proposition "all that is real is material" is true, then it is false; for such a universal idea is clearly not a material thing subject to sense verification. Thus, in the final analysis, there can be no theoretical proof or disproof of our freedom of choice.

However, while there is no theoretical contradiction in holding that one is determined, espousing such a position does involve one in a practical contradiction. For to hold that one's choices and actions are determined is to hold that one's choices and actions are not one's own. We know that we recognize options, that we deliberate, and that we put an end to deliberation through choice; in short, each one of us is conscious of having a self. This commonly recognized and accepted fact indicates that one cannot help but think of oneself as unique, irreducible to and hence, in some way, free from "the whole show." But if determinism is true, then really there is nothing but the whole show. There is no one home–not in the people I meet on the street, not in my friends, not in my loved ones, not in myself. But I am! I love! and I am loved!: such basic insights into fundamental human meaning (the insights of freedom) are incompatible with determinism.

Thus, while it is theoretically possible that my acts are all determined, existentially or practically, it is not possible for me to deny my ability to choose freely, that is, to deny that my acts are my acts. And while it may be possible to brazen it out, claiming that all that we think are free choices are not, such a stand is taken only at the cost of all meaningful activity: all my choices from what I shall have for breakfast, to whom I shall marry, to how I shall treat my friends and my neighbor and my children must, on such a hypothesis (and it is only a hypothesis) be no choices at all. If determinism is true, then life is absurd.

Since, on the one hand, it is difficult to account for self-awareness except on the assumption that we are free, and human activity is meaningful only if we are free; and since, on the other, there is no proof that we are not free: it is clear that there is no reason to doubt and every good reason to believe in our freedom of choice.

Now we are face-to-face with the main issue: how can providence and free will be simultaneously true of one human act? First of all, let us remember that God's way of knowing is not the same as the human way of knowing. If you ask whether I can know your future free actions, then the answer must be no. If you ask whether God can know your future free actions, then the answer must be yes. What is the difference? Human knowing is conditioned by time in the sense that particular states of affairs can only be known as past or present. I can know that my friend freely chose to go to Boston to see a show last week because I saw him there myself, or because I have heard through another friend that he was there, or because of some other acceptable evidence. We have no problem reconciling present certain knowledge with past free events. Likewise, if I see my friend greet an acquaintance of his, I know necessarily that he is doing so, although my

necessary knowledge has not in any way coerced him.
However, I do not know necessarily what my friend will
freely do tomorrow. If I did have necessary knowledge of
what he will do (because I rigged the situation), then his
action would not be free.

Why is the same thing not true for God's knowledge of
my free actions? How can God know what I shall do
tomorrow while not coercing me in any way to do it? It is
because God's knowledge is not related to the world the
same way that mine is. While I can have certain knowledge only of free acts that are present or past, or of future
determined actions, God has certain knowledge of even
future free acts–that is, acts that are future to us. For God
there is no future, or past. To God all is present. He does
not so much *foresee* what I shall do tomorrow as *see* what I
shall do. All time is present to God, for God is not in time.
If God were in time, then he would be in a position of
change, of becoming, of unfolding. But to become, one
must be imperfect and have something one may come to.
But God is perfectly actual; there is nothing into which he
could grow. A growing God would require something
existing prior to God, if not in time, then at least in perfection and hence dependence. But if this were true, then
God would not be the perfect cause of everything. For
this reason, Aquinas says that God is eternal, literally "not
temporal." The reason God knows with necessity what I
shall freely do tomorrow is because he sees in his eternal
present all things, past, present, and to come.

Consider the following analogy. There is a line of hikers
walking up a mountain path and a woman sitting at the
top of the mountain overlooking the path. The hikers in
the front of the line do not see what those coming after
are doing, but the woman sees all the hikers at once and
therefore knows with certainty what those at the head and

at the tail of the line are doing, even though their actions may be free. We who are in time are like the hikers and do not know what will freely happen in the future; but God, like the woman situated above the line of hikers, is above time and sees all events as they happen.

This does not sound too bad: God knows necessarily what I shall do because he sees me do it. God responds to my free actions. But this will not do. It cannot be that my actions cause God to know. That would be putting God in a passive position, making him subject to something else. But God is not subject to anything; as creator, all things are subject to him. We may like the idea of being able to affect God, for it satisfies our longing to exercise our freedom. But such an idea is false, and if we hold to such a position, we shall lose God. And to lose God is actually to place our freedom in jeopardy, as we shall see.

In God, knowing is the same as creating. Thus prior to my freely acting, God is the cause of my acting. The priority is not in time, for God is not in time, but it is a priority of dependence and origin. My free acts depend on God and have their origin in God. Thus, the model for how God's activity (providence) and my activity (free choice) operate simultaneously cannot be one in which God creates me as a kind of being with free will, and then leaves my choosing entirely up to me. It cannot be that in this one place in nature God steps back and allows something to happen outside his governance. Without God nothing happens. God creates; God conserves created things in being; and God moves things to action. There is no division of labor in which God does some things and I do others. God does everything, not in the sense that he does it all alone, but in the sense that without him, nothing can be or happen. Activities are real happenings; God is the cause of all that is real: therefore, God is the cause of activities. And a prior cause is more a cause than an instrumental cause. Just as it is true to say that the painter is more the cause of the picture than is the brush, so it is true to say that my free acts are more due to God than they are to me. But brushes are pushed around; presumably, if I am free, I am not pushed around. How then are my acts free and yet due to God?

The key to understanding this is to keep close to what we know about God's activity. We know that God is creator, that is, the cause of all things. Most things we know operate according to necessity, like atoms, trees, and animals insofar as they follow instinct. Human beings act freely. God is equally the cause of both what is necessitated and what is free. God makes things to be what they are, determined or free. His causality does not change natures; it makes natures. God's causality makes it necessary to say that determined things act of necessity and free things act freely. On God's providence Aquinas writes: "Just as when moving natural causes he does not take from them their natural activities, so also when he moves voluntary causes, he does not take from them the fact that their actions are voluntary, but rather he makes this very voluntariness in them; for he operates in each thing according to its proper nature."[3]

To repeat what I said above, we do not end up with a draw. The proper defense of the compatibility of divine providence and free will is not to say that God is the cause of everything else, but leaves rational creatures alone to make their own choices. If God were to leave us alone, we would cease to exist. If God were not to cause our movements of will, the will could not act; for the will is not always acting. It is the old boot-strap problem: a thing

---

[3]*Summa Theologiae* I, 83, 1 ad 3.

cannot give itself what it does not have. Nothing that is not already acting can bring itself to act. All imperfect activities, those which lack anything, depend ultimately on perfect activity; and perfect activity is what we mean by God. There are no fences between God and his creatures. A fence would be in the way of God's activity, something he did not want to be there, something independent of his will. But nothing is independent of God's will, which is the same as God's creating power. Besides this, a fence of independence from God's activity would not guarantee free activity, but, just the opposite, would mean the end of the activity.

Thus, God is the cause of every one of my activities. Some he causes through other things. For example, my body is affected by other material things. All matter acts on all matter through the universal law of gravity. My physical being is influenced by the entire order of the cosmos. On this point, Aquinas freely admits that certain emotional and personality traits of a person are influenced by the environment. My understanding may also be moved by another intellect within the universe. We see this happening every day: I do not know where Beacon Street in Boston is, and you tell me. Of course, it is not the whole activity of understanding that comes from another: if I did not think, then your explanation would not register. But the information which makes me know how to find Beacon street is caused by another. However, when we come to the rational will (the will as free), there is nothing in the universe which can directly move the will: the will is absolutely free. It is true that physical conditions and things such as suggestions and exhortations do affect us, but they are insufficient to move a free will to its act of choice. I may be hungry, and my friends may dare me to do it, but the decision to steal the peach from the grocer is an act of my free will. Of course, if I am completely ruled by my appetite or my friends so that I cannot even recognize the options or deliberate, then one could say that something else moved my will. But then it would be obvious to me that my free will did not operate in this case, and so there would be no violation of free will.

God alone moves the will to its free choice, and for this very reason the will is guaranteed to be free. No material thing can move the rational will, for the will is an immaterial faculty. As we noted above, all arguments to the contrary use reason and free choice and hence prove that the will is immaterial and free. Nor can another created immaterial thing, such as an angel, be the sufficient cause of the act of free choice. It may present objects or ideas to the intellect in order to persuade, but it is not able to move the will directly. Only the author of nature can be the direct cause of what is natural. If it is natural to the human being to have free will (and it is), then no other thing of nature can move that will, or the will would not be naturally free. Thus, freedom means to be free from the interference of some other thing. It cannot mean to be free from God, for freedom from God would be freedom from being: it would be nonexistence. God is not some other thing, an alternative force within the world which might interfere with human nature. Rather, he makes human nature to be free in its activity of choosing.

Thus, God turns out to be, not the threat to my freedom, but the absolute guarantor of my freedom. He alone, besides myself, causes the movements of my will. He makes it certain that nothing else causes my choices.[4] If God is thought of as the greatest force within the universe,

---

[4]The evil in my choice is a defect of something real, namely, reason, and so is not caused by God, but this is a topic for the next chapter.

then his prior action on my will would indeed mean that my will is not free. This is what is so important about Aquinas's insight into God as creator. God is not a force within the universe; he is the cause of the entire universe in all the ways in which we know the universe to be and operate. God causes determined things to operate under the determination of other things, and he causes free things to act free from all external determination. God's activity in all things of the universe is internal to them in such a way that it indistinguishable from their own activities. It is more intimate to them then they are to themselves. This is another way of saying that prior to the differentiated activities of things which make them different kinds of things is the cause that makes them be in the first place. It is not by chance or some lucky escape that we have free will in the face of God's providence. On the contrary, it is necessary that we have free will, since God makes us beings who have free will, and is the source for each act of free will. Whatever is real in my choices is caused by God.

Aquinas puts the mystery this way: God is wholly the cause of my free will, and I am wholly the cause of my free will. The idea of my will being partially due to me and partially due to God founders on the mistake of considering God as a part of this universe of things. God is, as it were, in another dimension; or better, he is in no dimension: for this reason his activity can be simultaneous with the activity of all things. Not only can it be simultaneous with the activity of all things, but it must be, for God is the reason that anything at all is and acts. So we must push the statement from the recognition that God does *not* violate the order of nature to the more surprising recognition that without God operating, all nature would be violated in the sense of ceasing to exist. Nor does

God's activity apply just to the existence of things. Without God's operation, no existing thing could operate, not
even free will. In the words of Aquinas: "It is also clear
that the same effect is not attributed to a natural cause and
to divine power as if it were partly from God, and partly
from the natural agent; rather, it is totally from each,
according to a different way, just as the same effect is
totally attributed to the instrument and also totally to the
principal agent."[5]

The truth that God's providence is not an alternative to
human freedom removes a misgiving (based on a misunderstanding) about providence. Providence is often
understood as the same thing as fate when, in fact, concerning human actions, it is quite the opposite. Many
people rebel (quite rightly) at the idea of God controlling
us in such a way that we have no say in whether our lives
are ultimately happy and meaningful or not. The Reformation interpretation of providence and predestination
which informs much of Western Culture has much to do
with this. In this interpretation, we are saved or damned
regardless of what we do. We are absolutely subject to
God, passive under his ruling hand. In one way, of
course, this is true since we and all things are created from
nothing and moved to our activities by God. But in an
extremely important way, this is not true. And its untruth
has had serious repercussions in our understanding of the
relationship between human activities and God. On the
model of providence as fate, as what must be done, we are
viewed as helpless and inconsequential in the determination of our ultimate end. There is nothing to do but trust
God, passively accepting what God wills to be done with
us. We are not free but determined to be saved or

---

5 *Summa Contra Gentiles* III, 70, [8].

damned. What appear to be choices of ours are merely a facade for God's activity of providence. We are players in a play, acting out our predetermined parts. It is the glory of most who have followed the lead of the Reformers on predestination that they have not succumbed to the implications of this position. They remain actively engaged in their lives, living as if their actions made some difference.

For Thomas Aquinas, our actions do make a difference. It is true that God is the cause of all my actions, but so am I. Since God is not an alternative to me but the cause of me, his activity does not preclude mine, but upholds it. The actions I perform are wholly done by God and wholly done by me. They are not done by me despite being done by God; rather, their being done by me depends on their being done by God. Trusting in God, on this model, is not a collapse, a relaxation of engagement in the face of futile toil. To trust God is in no way to cease to care (except in the sense of useless, irrational worry). It does not in any way remove me from my obligations to know the truth and to do what is good. For God is not an alternative to my life in the sense of offering me an alternative mode of action. I must continue to act as a human being, for that is what God's activity makes me. To trust in God's providence is not to give in with a sigh to the inevitable; it is, on the contrary, to focus on the real directives and demands of being human. We cannot fall back on God's providence as an external principle to guide us, for we do not know what God's providence in particular is. To live according to providence is not to cease acting, "to go along for the ride," but to begin to act, to begin to live a truly free and human life.

Correcting this misunderstanding of what God's providence means removes the grounds for the existential atheist's rejection of God as the great oppressor of human freedom. Although one might tend to think that if God were not the direct cause of my free will, then it would have more chance to be free, just the opposite proves to be true. Separating the activity of free will from God by intermediaries would precisely render free will unfree. The atheist's mistake is to conceive of God as being an overwhelming force which infringes on one's freedom. He is right to reject such a God, but he has not rejected the true God who is the creator of all that exists, including human freedom. God is not the biggest bully on the block from whom protection is best assured by putting as many people as possible between myself and him, hoping he will not notice me and leave me alone. Rather he is the protector from all bullies. God alone is the cause of free will. He will not allow any other creature to interfere; he could not and still create a creature with free will.

In trying to show how God can be the all-powerful creator and mover of all things while, nevertheless, not manipulating them like a puppeteer, there is a danger that we may reduce him in our minds to an inconceivable, vapid being. It is important to combat this danger. While it is true that God is inconceivable, he is anything but vapid. It may seem, at first, that such a God as Aquinas suggests to us is not very interesting, that he is rather undistinguished, that he does not do very much. After all, in the Chapter Two we said that God does *not* interfere with the laws of nature, and now we are saying that God does *not* interfere in human actions. He certainly does not seem very useful or impressive, for when we know what we can know about him, we have little to apply to the world. One may get the feeling that God is powerless, that he does not make any difference to the world, perhaps even that he does not care about the world. But we must not let this impression dominate our thinking. We may know little about God, but what we do know, we must not let be clouded by vague feelings of dissatisfaction or bewilderment.

God makes all the difference, for God is the reason why there is any world at all, and also the ultimate reason for all the activities that go on in the world, including the four great forces of material reality and free choice of the will. But precisely because we know God to be the cause of everything, we know that he cannot be any kind of nature or cause on the model of the causes which we recognize in this world. If God were a particular kind of cause (albeit the most powerful), we still would not have the answer to our ultimate question. There would still be the additional question to ask: "What is the explanation for the context in which this cause is related to other causes?" In short, we would not have God, but an angel or a force of nature, or something of the kind.

God can be the universal creating and provident cause of everything only because he is not a particular kind of thing. As long as there are kinds of things or causes, there remains the further issue of why there are many things which yet share a common context. The explanation or cause of the context cannot be part of the context. Thus God is not part of the universe of things whose existence he explains. And it is only because he is not a thing of a determinate nature that he can operate at the heart of everything without distorting its nature. Consider an analogy taken from the world of light and color. It is only because sunlight is not itself a particular color that it can bring forth the colors of all things. If it were red, then, rather than bringing forth the natural colors of things, it would distort them: red would look pink; pink would look white; orange would look yellow, etc. In a similar way, it is only because God is not a particular kind of thing that he brings forth the operations of all things. If we consider God as a particular thing, then his activity in other things would be an addition of a particular kind and hence would indeed distort them, skewing their natures. But God is the cause of natures, and so he cannot himself be one nature among them.

This is not to say that God lacks the fundamental principle of reality which we call nature in a thing. Whatever reality there is in the effect must preexist in the cause. God is not less real, but more real that the things he has created. It is simply that we do not and cannot conceive, by an act of natural reason, the reality that is God. Every idea we have of God fixes God as a finite being among other beings; and we cannot help but do this when we try to conceive of God because our minds are attuned to know the natures of the material things of this world. However, when we know that God is creator from an analysis of these material things, we know him to be the cause of all finite things. If God is the cause of all finite things, then he himself cannot be a finite thing. One thing we can be sure of is that our finite ideas of God must always be false. Every conception of God loses God by making God finite, which is to be a creature and not the creator. And by losing God to nature in this way we lose nature. God the creator guarantees that each nature is what it is; that God is creator does not add anything to the nature of created beings. But bring God into the world of things as the most powerful force among them, and God's presence to things would then mean adding something to their natures, thus changing them. To demote God from creator to the great power of the universe is to give up the certainty of nature, including human nature with its free will.

Thus, although it is true that we cannot conceive of what God is, this is not the end of the road for reason: rather, it is the ever-renewing point of departure. We only know God the creator to exist from our study of the things of the world. Our study of these things leads us to say that they are all caused to exist by one transcendent cause. As the cause of all things, God can hardly be powerless or contentless or unreal. All the reality and activity of things pre-exists in him, or he could never create them.

Knowing that God is creator, however, is a key to knowing the universe and human freedom in a way that we did not expect. Instead of handing our knowledge of the world to us in a neat and tidy package signed "From God," this key is a litmus test by which we can tell whether we are being true to the nature of creation. The minute we find ourselves using God to prove something about physics or free will, we know we are misusing God and mucking up natural reason. The knowledge that God exists and that he is all-provident does not replace the natural knowledge we may have of the world with a more perfect and complete knowledge of the world. God does not push creation around, as if he were the motor that drives it; he lets it be what it is; he gives it existence. It is not, nor can ever be, the case that when we know the nature of God we know the nature of things. This is, perhaps, the most difficult point of all to grasp: if we think we know the nature and activity of God, then we will mistake the nature and activity of things. There is, of course, the Christian position that the blessed know the nature of God and through knowing God know all things. I am not denying this; but this knowledge is not naturally attainable by us; if we get it, it will be because God, through an act of grace, gives it to us.

In this life, we can never attain to the knowledge of what God is. This is true even for faith. Aquinas writes: "Through the revelation of grace in this life we do not know of God what he is, and thus we are united to him as if to one unknown."[6] Since we do not know what God is, if we argue that such and such a thing is so because God is so and so, we are only succeeding in destroying the truth. Every time we argue from God's nature to the natures of things, we are arguing in an illegitimate fashion. A conception of God's nature gets in the way of knowing things, for that conception must always be false.

It was a conception of God as all-powerful, when brought into conjunction with the human activity of choice, that led the Reformers to deny free will in the face of God's providence. Since, if you are the cause of my actions (through hypnotism or propaganda or whatever), I am not free, the Reformers thought that God's causality makes me unfree. But they were wrong here precisely because they understood God's activity to be like man's. Every conception of God limits him to our way of being and acting. "My ways are not your ways, says the Lord."

Knowing that God is, but that we do not know his nature, protects God's creation. If one wants to know what things are, one must consider them. To know God as creator (which is not to have an idea of God) is to know that his creatures are worth knowing in themselves. He did not make them because he needed them, but so that they might exist. Not only does Aquinas's warning against adherence to a false conception of God allow for the possibility of knowing things, it also protects the way to knowing God himself better, since our way to God is

---

[6]*Summa Theologiae* I, 12, 13 ad 1.]

through things, and a misunderstanding of things can only distort our understanding of God.

In sum, a false conception of God (and any idea that God is such and such is one) cuts off the way to the truth. It is bad for science, and bad for theology. Here we see the heroism of reason in freeing God from the world, thus guaranteeing both a living God and a world in which science and freedom may thrive. Reason here is the dragon-slayer, destroying false images of God, images which debase God and human activities. In the name of God, all sorts of atrocities have been committed. We must understand that we cannot use God to justify our activities. Our freedom and responsibility are given us by God to be used, not to be sacrificed to an idol in the form of our idea of God.

How then should we proceed? We must attend to the things that we can know: to the material things around us, and to our own humanity. A proper grasp of what it means to call God creator guarantees the fecundity of philosophy in the broad sense–the pursuit of all wisdom. God is mystery, even to the natural understanding. There is not one God of Revelation who is mysterious, and another of philosophy who is perfectly clear. Reason, no less that faith, proclaims God to be mystery. But mystery is not meaninglessness: rather, it is a deeper meaning which invites one to reason, which feeds the life of the mind. To think about God is to think ever more deeply, to extend into mystery–into that which is not yet understood. It is to go beyond old meaning, not into absurdity, but greater clarity. Even the process of saying what God is not, which we have said is the best we can do in this life, is not without growth in knowledge. If you explain to me what a lemur is by saying that it is not an inanimate thing, that it is not a plant, that it is not cold-blooded, that it is not a bird, then, although I do not know the essence of lemur, I have learned something. I have learned to avoid mistaking a lemur for any of the things rejected. So too, when we say of God that he is not material, not in time, not finite, not caused, we are learning to avoid mistakes about what God is. While we can never by natural reason or faith know what God's essence is, we nevertheless learn something about him from studying his effects, and understanding what these effects require as their cause.

To raise up as first principle any finite expression of the finite human mind, in other words, to use the word God to refer to what we can comprehend, is to stultify the life of the mind. It is as if to say that meaning has once and forever been achieved and all questions answered. It is to kill the wonder which feeds reason. Aquinas's notion of God guarantees that this will not happen, for God is not to be understood as an opponent to his creation and, in particular, to human beings in their activity of choosing. It might make sense to speak of some other created thing as an opponent, something which shared a common world with us, but it cannot make any sense to consider God as one, for he makes this world and hence is not in the world in competition with his creatures. It is precisely *because* God is not a part of this fabric of nature that he can act in nature without violating it.

Not only do providence and free will prove, in the end, to be compatible, they turn out to be the closest of allies, linked together inseparably in our proper understanding of each. We have seen that God is the absolute guarantor of free will. Our free will is also the best model we have for understanding what God could be like. When we think about why God would create, we can come up with no reason for this, in the sense of coming up with something that could require God to create. Likewise, when

we think about why we make a free choice, we can think
of no reason why we must make that choice. Unlike the
understanding which is dependent upon what is known
and, to that extent, passive, the activity of free choice is
wholly active, since it brings something new into being,
something that did not have to be. We must not conceive
God out of being God. Our awareness of our free will, if
we would but pay attention to it, guarantees that we shall
not make this mistake. We cannot conceive of free will
any more that we can conceive of God. Yet we know that
we have free will, and we know that God exists. If we
wish to consider the activity of God with the least falsifi-
cation, let us consider our free actions which are also his.

This is indeed a wonder to be pondered, and it is reason
which has brought us to this mystery. Reason tells us that
there is a creating God who, as creator, is also the
omniscient and all-powerful governor of his creation.
Reason tells us that there is no good argument against free
will and that the whole world of meaningful activities and
relationships argues for our freedom to choose. Thus, reason tells us that God is the whole cause of my free choice
(since he is the whole cause of the existence of the universe), and I am the whole cause of my free choice (since I
am obviously free). In human freedom, there is nothing at
work but God and human being. Since there are no intermediaries, we can be sure that here we meet God's activity most directly. And what do we find? We find an
existing human being choosing freely, no more, not
freedom distorted by God, and no less, a creature enjoying
real existence by the grace of God.

$\mathcal{V}$
God and Morality

Thomas Aquinas says that providence is the rational plan of God for his creation. In the last chapter we showed that this plan does not take away human freedom, but on the contrary, assures it. In this chapter I would like to pursue the question of what such a providence positively implies for us in terms of ethics. If God has a rational plan for human beings, what can we say about it? What does God's providence mean for us in terms of directing our lives? Two models come readily to mind. One suggests a detailed plan which God imposes on our actions. This model obviously will not do because it takes away the human freedom which we said providence guarantees. If what we do is imposed on us, then we do not do it freely. A second model would have us reading this plan from the mind of God and following it. This avoids the denial of free will, but it presupposes that we can know what God's plan is. However, to know God's plan we must know his nature which we have said is impossible for natural reason. But perhaps, even if it is impossible for natural reason, it is possible for faith: to be good is to do what the Bible tells us. We can know God's will through Revelation. This third position has its own problems. Although it allows for freedom and some access to what God wills, accepting it means accepting the position that ethics is merely a matter of faith. But if one makes the requirements of morality a matter of faith, then those who do not share the faith (which is a matter of grace not nature) will not be obliged by any of the rules found in Revelation. This seems inappropriate, to say the least. Just because it says "Do not kill" in the Bible, this does not mean that unbelievers are free to kill. Why not? Where is the source of the human obligation to be good?

This is the puzzle that forms the center of this chapter: how is it that God and morality are related? If one is a materialist, there is no great problem, for the materialist does not think that there is a God nor that there are any absolute values. The assumption that all real things are material excludes the reality of an immaterial source of everything; and it excludes the reality of absolute unchanging values, since no one has ever seen or weighed such things as justice or generosity. The problem is really one for theism, whether philosophical or religious. If one claims that God exists as the cause of everything and claims that there are absolute moral standards which we are required to respect, it seems a plausible move to say that these standards depend on God and that we know them either by knowing God or by accepting, through faith, his Revelation of them. If we say this, and it turns out that we cannot know God naturally and that faith is a gift from God not owed to us naturally, then what happens to the foundations for ethics? Does the one who lacks the gift of faith have any obligations at all?

This is a very live issue today. A great part of the modern world, influenced by the thought of Friedrich Nietzsche and Sigmund Freud (among others), assumes that objective moral norms are inventions of religion, and that traditional morality is a matter of superstition imposed through means of inventive fantasies of God, sin, and salvation, for the purpose of keeping the "herd" in line. Traditionally, as this position would have it, people have been moral upright merely because they feared the punishments threatened by religion and hoped for the promised rewards for doing what God said was right. All we really want is to gratify our libido, to satisfy the drives of our animality, for that is all we are–animals. Along with this animal drive is a desire for power, to dominate, to have things one's own way. All talk about an immortal soul and God is empty dreaming. When God is recognized as an illusion, the structure of absolute moral standards disappears, and what is left is the drive for sexual fulfillment and the will to power. If I do not believe in God, then I am not bound by the petty morality that religion demands.

Now in a strange way, the ancient tradition handed down from Plato and Aristotle and incorporated into Christian thought lends support to such an interpretation of the foundation of ethical obligation: for Plato and Aristotle equated the pinnacle of human activity with the contemplation of the divine. This is the best life, absolutely. In fact, human happiness is seen as becoming divine as far as possible. Divinity is what is really good. If one denies that God exists, as did Nietzsche and Freud, then the pinnacle of goodness and guarantee of unchanging values evaporates, and with it disappears the source of human happiness and ethical obligation.

Oddly enough, it is a Christian philosopher and theologian, an intellectual disciple of Plato and Aristotle, who corrects this model of the relation between God and morality that Nietzsche and Freud reject. Aquinas agrees that if we hold moral obligation to be real simply because we believe that God said so, then morality has no natural human universality, and unbelievers need not respect it. Through a deeper understanding of what constitutes the human good, and a deeper understanding of God as creator, Aquinas steers his way clear to having an ethics based on reason and human nature and a God whose presence to human beings does not spell an abrogation of their humanity. Thus, to the challenge which says that there can only be human moral obligation if we have an idea of God as the highest good and sole worthy object of human attention and contemplation (whether by natural reason or faith), Aquinas replies that there can only be human morality and happiness if we have *no* idea of God–that is, if we understand God to be creator. For God as creator is not a principle of ethical obligation over and above human nature and specifically different from it, but the maker of human nature and its principles of obligation. It is not that God does not matter to morality. Without God the creator there would be no humanity to be obliged. But it is also true that if we think of God as the highest thing in the universe, which can be contemplated as an alternative to human goods, then there could be no *human* morality at all. All human perfection, on this view, lies in becoming divine. To unfold how it is that Aquinas handles this issue, let us begin with his simplest notion of what it is to be ethical. Then we shall distinguish this notion from the positions of the materialists. Finally, we shall see how it goes beyond even the thinking of his masters and allies in the rejection of materialism, Plato and Aristotle.

Aquinas says that ethics is a matter of being happy. If one were happy, one would be good. This sounds a bit surprising and perhaps shocking. We are used to hearing that if one would be happy, then one must be good; but to turn the terms around does not sound right. Yet for Aquinas happiness and the ethical life are one and the same; and, to make this point absolutely clear, I have presented the equation by reversing the traditional order of the terms. Simply put, the requirement of God's providence for us is that we be happy.[1] The divine law prescribes only what will fulfill us as human beings, only what will make us good and happy. Happiness, that is, the ethical life, would have to be something we want, or otherwise it would be contrary to free will. And it would have to be something obvious, so that it would be present to all in the immediate way in which we said God's providence must operate in all his creatures.

But having said that the ethical life is the happy life, we have only cleared the way for the much greater task of untangling what the word "happy" means when equated with the ethical life. For in saying that the happy life is the best one for human beings, we have only restated what nearly all philosophers have said, and yet these philosophers disagree rather vociferously on what human happiness is. Perhaps the most obvious meaning of the word "happiness," one ingrained in us in so far as we are

---

[1] Notice the difference between providence and fate, here. One would never speak of fate as a requirement, something that we ought to do. Fate is what we cannot avoid. But God's plan acting in us (providence) is also our activity, as we said in the last chapter. Although providence is not indeed something we can frustrate, our relation to it is not one of passive resignation, but of free and active participation. God's presence to us makes us free and reasonable and, therefore, obliges us to act in certain ways.

animals, is pleasure and freedom from pain. This is the meaning happiness naturally has for young children, and the one it often has (although unnaturally, as I shall explain) for adults. The best life is the one full of pleasure and free of pain. Such a view of happiness is logically tied to a materialistic view of reality, and those philosophers ancient and modern who are materialists generally hold such an ethics, at least if they are consistent. Of ancient philosophers, the Epicureans and the atomists held such an ethical position. The Stoics had a more refined, if less consistent, theory in which they considered mental pleasures of higher worth than sensual pleasures and therefore shunned the pleasures of the flesh.

In the modern world, emotivists (who claim that ethics is a matter of feeling), utilitarians (who claim that the good act is the act that brings the most pleasure to the most people), and social contract theorists (who claim that out of self-interest we decide to restrict our aggressive actions, if others will do the same, and agree to live by conventional rules) all regard the gaining of pleasure and the avoidance of pain as the foundations of a happy life. David Hume, Jeremy Bentham, and Thomas Hobbes are the modern founders of these respective theories. I say *modern* founders because these theories were held by people in the ancient world and are, in fact, perennial options for the meaning of the ethical life.[2]

A fundamental principle shared by adherents to emotivism, utilitarianism, and social contract theory is that all that is real is material. With the Renaissance and the divorce of reason from faith came the tendency to equate immaterial reality with faith and material reality with

---

[2]Epicurius, for example, was something of a utilitarian, and several of those who converse with Socrates in the Platonic dialogues were either emotivists or social contract theorists.

what can be naturally known. Here is, in brief, the argument followed, in one way or another, by all the modern philosophers who hold that pleasure and pain are the principles of ethics. All that is real can be verified by the senses; justice and injustice, generosity and greed, good and evil have never been seen, heard, touched or otherwise verified by the senses: therefore, these standards of morality are not real, and the command to follow them is meaningless. Pleasure and pain, on the other hand, belong to us insofar as we are physical. They can be verified by sense experience, and therefore can be said to be the real guides of all our behavior. Such an argument assumes the absolute validity of the scientific method with its explicit materialism, as well as the method's claim to be the sole road to truth.

The only problem with such an argument for the foundations of ethics (and, therefore, with the theories which are based on it) is that its assumed first principle is false. Materialism is not true, and therefore conclusions drawn from this first principle need not be true. The mistake most modern ethical thinkers have made is to assume that the scientific method is the *only* true one. But as you recall, the truth of the scientific method cannot itself be verified by sense experience, and the claim for the universality of materialism implies the use of the immaterial faculty of reason.

There have been, of course, exceptions to materialism throughout history. Plato and Aristotle are not among the ancient philosophers who equate happiness with pleasure. They claim that the good life is the happy life, but they do not read human happiness in terms of pleasure. Among the modern philosophers of the Renaissance and Enlightenment, Kant is conspicuous for his rejection of pleasure as the ultimate human good. And by and large, the medieval tradition stemming from Augustine to Aquinas is also firm in its refusal to equate happiness with pleasure. All these philosophers say that pleasure cannot be *human* fulfillment because it is not what specifically characterizes human beings. It is true that pleasure is the good of animals, but human beings are not just animals: they are *rational* animals. Thus, human fulfillment or happiness must involve reason at its center.

I said above that the first meaning of happiness is pleasure; this actually is untrue, for pleasure is not meaningful. Pleasure operates automatically according to material conditions. If it is pleasure that guides us, then we are not free, for to be run by material conditions is to be determined. But it certainly seems as if we choose pleasure; and if pleasure is chosen, then it must be meaningful. This, however, is a false impression. If pleasure and pain are our only guides, then we do not choose them, for choice is a matter of recognizing intelligible good and pursuing it. If we choose pleasure and pain, it is only because we consider them to contain intelligible and meaningful good; and, if we do that, we are making a mistake. A famous utilitarian philosopher, John Stuart Mill, wrestles with this problem of the intelligibility of pleasure. He says that human happiness is not like the happiness of a pig, because we pursue higher kinds of pleasure. The pleasure of knowing and acting freely is better than the pleasure of satisfied appetite. Aside from the problem of what judges one pleasure to be better than another (pleasure cannot do it since it is being judged), is it true that we seek to know and to act reasonably only in order to get pleasure?

This is simply the question whether there are any other things that guide our actions beside pleasure. If we find that there is anything at all that we value aside from pleasure, then it will be clear that pleasure is not the only legitimate motive of our actions. Aristotle says that pleasure is not the only reason for our acting, and beyond this that it is not the reason for *any* human action. Consider knowledge: do we like to know simply because it brings us pleasure, or is there anything about knowing that we value for its own sake? Certainly knowing can bring us pleasure: to know that a good friend is coming to visit me tomorrow fills me with pleasure; to find the answer to a problem that has been puzzling him for weeks pleases the mathematician. So it seems clear that pleasure results from knowledge. But can we say that knowing matters *only* because of the pleasure it brings? Aristotle says absolutely not; on the contrary, the pleasure depends wholly on the knowing. It is true enough that each human activity carries with it pleasure when it is done well. This is because we are unities of mind and matter. Even a specifically immaterial activity like knowing is the act of the whole human being and so affects the body. However, if there is pleasure in knowing, it is not because knowing is reducible in value to pleasure, but because the knowing activity itself is done well. Focus on the pleasure and one will lose the knowing, and hence the pleasure. The surest way of getting the answer to a problem wrong is to concern oneself with the pleasure of knowing and not the evidence proper to knowing.

Consider another dimension of our human choosing –friendship. Is friendship good because it brings pleasure? Is pleasure the only reason for friendship? Friendship, like knowledge, is a human activity that carries with it its own pleasure. One can only have the pleasure of friendship if one has the activity of having a friend. Friendship cannot be secondary in importance to pleasure as a means is to an end. In a means-to-end situation, the value of the means depends on the value of the end. But the pleasure derived from friendship depends on the activity of friendship, not vice versa. The surest way to lose friendship (and hence the pleasure that goes along with it) is to seek *my* pleasure in the friendship and not the friendship itself.

In a way, this conclusion is immediately evident to us. We understand that knowledge and friendship are not synonymous with pleasure. They require a dedication to activity and to caring, while pleasure is something that happens to us, not something we do. For this reason, Aristotle and Aquinas insist that properly human activities, activities requiring free choice, are never guided by pleasure. They are guided by goods which are known to be good by reason. To the extent that pleasure dominates our pursuit of these goods, they are imperfectly achieved. Pleasure, as motive, represents the unthinking, the determined: to the extent that pleasure dominates our actions, the actions are not free, and hence not specifically human. If pleasure were to dominate us completely, *human* actions would cease.

It is interesting to consider, for a moment, the ideal of happiness that seems to dominate our modern culture, the ideal that says that human happiness is vacation. We work so that we can make money so that we can take a vacation–ideally, a permanent vacation. I know that this is a vast generalization, but it is, at least, the ubiquitous advertising-magazine image our society portrays of human happiness. Such a position is, of course, quite compatible with the theory that human happiness lies in pleasure, and so the ideal has plenty of support from those philosophers we have mentioned who take pleasure and pain as the first principles of ethics. But it has no support, alas, from reason. It is a curious coincidence that the root of the word "vacation" is the Latin *vacare* which means "to empty." The life of pleasure is the vacation

life–a life empty of reason, of freedom, of meaning. This is
not to say that all vacations are meaningless or that leisure
time is necessarily empty. A vacation to rest from activities so that one may pursue these activities in a more fulfilling way, a vacation to restore the wonder at life by
appreciating the beauty of nature or seeing and learning
something new, a vacation to deepen a friendship or pursue an interest in art or some skill: all these are legitimate
human activities that are not only ethically allowable, but
commendable. But the ideal of a vacation life as an escape
from activity into passive reception of pleasure, of empty-
headedness as a permanent condition, is a rejection of
meaning and specifically human living. Such a life, pursued in its pure form, would differ little from the life of a
drug addict or an alcoholic. Pleasure is addictive, but that
to which it binds us is not happiness in any meaningful
sense, but a drift away from human activities–from
knowledge, friendship, beauty, and freedom.

Happiness, then, is not pleasure. What is it? Aquinas
gives two apparently very different answers to this question. Sometimes he speaks of happiness as a life involved
in pursuing human goods like knowledge, family, friendship, and beauty. At other times he says our happiness
lies in contemplating God. These versions of happiness
certainly sound like alternatives: the first is a matter of
natural human activities; the second is the supernatural
activity of contemplating God. If human happiness is
only achieved in the gift of God's showing himself to us,
then what happens to human happiness in the sense of
fulfilling the ethical requirements naturally placed on *all*
human beings–believers and nonbelievers alike? Morality
seems to be absorbed by faith, in which case those without
faith are not under any obligation, and human activities
are not ultimately meaningful in themselves. Let us look

at the two answers in themselves first, and then see what can be said for their relationship.

Aquinas says, following Plato and Aristotle, that every human action aims at some good. Whatever we do by free choice is done in order to achieve something we consider valuable. Thus, there is a first principle of action which we cannot help but follow: good is to be done and promoted and evil avoided. This is not yet an ethical requirement, but a statement about how we in fact do act when we choose freely. Even the murderer seeks a good, whether the good of money, security, revenge or whatever. This is not to say that these are real goods, but they appear to be good to him or he would not choose them. Ethics, properly speaking, has to do with sorting out the real from the apparent goods.

The reason why the first most general principle of action does not give us ethics is because it has no content. It does not tell us whether or not there are goods which we ought not to pursue because they destroy other more basic goods. Are there some goods which are fundamental to human well-being? Are there any universal human goods which all human beings recognize as basic and which are always to be promoted and never violated? Aquinas suggests three basic goods which coincide with basic human inclinations. The obligation to respect these goods he calls the natural law. First, we have a natural inclination to live which we understand as fundamental to human happiness. Second, we have a natural desire to procreate and raise a family which we recognize as basic to human well-being. Third, we have a natural inclination to pursue knowledge and social life. We understand immediately, through being human, that these goods are fundamental to our well-being. We value life; we value family (insofar,

in part, as we value life, for family is how life comes to be);
we value knowledge and the things that are appropriate
to life in society, such as friendship, organizations, games
of play and skill, and artistic endeavors. No one has to
prove to us that these things are valuable. As soon as we
are able to reflect on what it is to be human, we recognize
that these things are good. They are to be promoted and
not violated wherever they are found, whether in me or in
others. Reason, as we said in Chapter Three, has the ability to universalize; it transcends time and place. Therefore, reason does not say these are good *for me*, but good *in
themselves*. The reason that recognizes these fundamental
goods knows that they are true universally, for all human
beings, forever.

That these goods are basic is self-evident: we recognize
immediately that they are good, with no uncertainty.
What is good for everyone at all times and in all places
ought always to be pursued and never violated. There
could never be a time when some more basic value might
overrule these. These basic goods are the first principles of
all ethical behavior–the ultimate starting points for moral
obligation. They are the obvious outlines of what full
human happiness means. If we violate these goods, we
violate what we value; we destroy what we consider to be
ultimately worthwhile; we are in contradiction–valuing
and disvaluing the same thing at the same time. This is to
be absurd in our actions; this is to be immoral. To be
immoral is to be unhappy; it is not getting what one really
wants. Happiness is a life lived in accord with these basic
values, and unhappiness is a life spent in violation of
these values. Thus, the person who is rich, comfortable,
famous, well-respected and powerful but has become so
by lying, or cheating, or betraying friends, or some other

violation of the basic goods, is unhappy, no matter what he himself or the world might say to the contrary.

Although in many ways in agreement with Plato and Aristotle, this position of Aquinas is really quite different from the teaching of Plato, and also departs significantly from Aristotle. Plato had taught that virtue is knowledge and vice is ignorance. If one only knew what the right thing was to do, then one would do it. One is bad only because one is ignorant. Against this, Aquinas is saying that one is only wrong when one knows what is the right thing to do, but still does the opposite. Prerequisite to immorality is knowing what is right. For this reason we do not account children and the insane responsible for their actions. There is , of course, an element of knowledge required for one to be virtuous, but the knowledge does not guarantee right action but only makes departure from its rule an immoral act.

Aristotle attempts to answer the question of why one may act against reason by developing an ethics based on virtue as habit. By repeated actions we develop character traits that are hard to break. If we are used to giving in to pleasure, then, although we may know that pleasure is not as great a good as friendship, we may sacrifice friendship for pleasure in a pinch. On the other hand, if one is used to telling the truth, then, when one is in a tight spot where a response must be given quickly, one will likely tell the truth rather than lie to save one's reputation, or for monetary advantage, or for whatever might be at stake. Where do we get the guidance to develop good habits? We look to the actually virtuous person, and imitate. How does the actually virtuous person know what is right? Aristotle says that the actually virtuous person is guided by right reason, but he never says what the content of this right reason is.

Aquinas fills in this gap in Aristotle's ethics. He says that the guide to moral action is the natural law which is immediately accessible to each person, since each person has direct access to the principles of reason. It is true that we may become good by imitating the good person, but we recognize the good person, in the first place, because we know what it means to be good. That we all naturally value life, friendship, knowledge, art, and self-determination as basic human goods is the basis for obligation. We must not disvalue what we value. Thus, Aquinas pinpoints obligation by spelling out what is implied in Aristotle's notion of right reason.

The second way Aquinas has of speaking of human happiness is to say that it consists in the contemplation of God. Philosophically, he inherits this idea from Plato and Aristotle, and it is, of course, compatible with the Christian notion of equating ultimate happiness with the beatific vision–God's gift of himself which Christians believe God will grant in heaven to those who are saved. Plato, as you will recall, says that the human being is the rational soul. He also says that the rational soul is a spark of the divine. For Plato, to be happy is to remember that one is divine, to leave behind what specifies one as human and rejoin divinity.

Aristotle takes another route, but ultimately ends up where Plato does. He argues that theoretical contemplation of the divine is a higher activity than moral virtue. His argument goes as follows. Human happiness lies in activity. Reason is the highest activity we perform; God is the highest possible object for this activity: therefore, perfect human happiness lies in the contemplation of God. Argued in such a way, this sounds like God is an alternative to other good human activities. For Aristotle, I think it was. Recall that Aristotle's God is self-thinking thought and not the creator of all things. This God is not thinking about us, and is not, therefore, thinking about what is good for us. For this reason, to know God is not at all to know human goods, but rather divine good. Ultimate happiness for Aristotle is to become divine as far as is possible, as opposed to being human. Recall also what we said in Chapter Three about Aristotle's ultimate conclusion about reason. For Aristotle, reason transcends what it is to be human. It is our visitor and guide while we live, but returns to its source when we die. The moral virtues, such as courage and justice, are properly human, for they involve embodied action in a social context. Contemplation, however, which Aristotle considers the highest virtue and the activity of the best life, is pure theoretical reason involved with divine things; that is, it is reason knowing itself. This highest "human" happiness turns out not to be really human at all, but divine. Thus, like Plato, Aristotle holds happiness to be equivalent with divinity–reason (which is divine) contemplating itself.

Aquinas does say, with Plato and Aristotle, that contemplation of God is ultimate happiness, but he means something quite different. In the first place, it is impossible for us to know God's essence by nature, or even by faith, in this life. By natural reason we can never know what God is, but only what he is not. By faith we do not know what God is, but are joined with him as to something unknown. If we cannot know God's essence, then that essence itself cannot naturally move the will to seek it.

For Aquinas, it is the basic goods which naturally move the human will. However, to say this is not to rule out God, for God is not an alternative to the goods human beings can pursue, but the perfection of such goods. No one completely fulfills the activity of knowledge; no one completely fulfills the activity of art; no one completely fulfills the activity of friendship. The basic goods themselves are not intrinsically finite; they are never perfectly enacted by any one person, nor by all people together. The basic goods are infinite. God is infinite. I am not, of course, equating the basic goods with God, for they are human goods, and they are not all the goods there are; but they do not differ from God as the unworthy differs from the worthy. They do not block our way to God by being bad for us. God, as the creator and perfector of our nature, wills for us only what is good for us. He wills that our human nature be perfected, not replaced. Aquinas writes: "God is only offended by us when we act against our own good."[3] The fundamental human goods do not need to be cast aside in favor of God. Thus, when Aquinas says that God is "the aggregate of all good things" or "the universal good" or "all that the will desires," he is not denying the goodness of human goods.

Again, the reason Aquinas is not really saying the same thing as Plato and Aristotle, when he says that our happiness lies in contemplating God, is because Aquinas's God is not the God of Plato or Aristotle. For Aquinas, to contemplate God is to be *humanly* fulfilled, not, like Plato and Aristotle, to become divine. The creature/creator distinction can never be removed. As creator, God does not require that we his creatures turn from natural human goods (I mean basic human goods now) to another good, but that we pursue, and promote, and perfect the goods that are essential to being human. The basic goods are ultimate ends, not means to a further end which is God. Even in heaven there is no reason to believe that human goods will be replaced. While it is true that in the beatific

---

[3]*Summa Contra Gentiles* III, 122, [2].

vision we will not *need* particular friends, beautiful works of art, knowledge of special sciences (since we shall be given them by the grace of God) the basic goods of friendship, beauty, and knowledge will not be rendered obsolete. The basic goods will still be *valued*. The meaning of human ethical fulfillment will not be changed (although it will be perfected), for the heart of ethics lies in this valuing, in the intention and motive behind any act, not in any particular exterior action. On this point, Aquinas himself writes: "Activities of a moral nature are called good or evil on account of the rational end (intention)."4 As to the relationship between intentional acts of the will and exterior acts in ethics, Aquinas is quite clear: "Exterior acts have the character of morality only to the extent that they are voluntary."5

What is essential to something is what makes that thing to be what it is. Now intention or motive has this central place in our actions. If the intention is good, the act is a good act; if the intention is bad, the act is always a bad action. By good intention, I do not mean a good feeling or a generally benevolent attitude, but the use of reason operating carefully to understand and judge what is right and wrong. Since the essence of ethics is the value intended and not the physical action, the cessation of the need for physical action is not the cessation of ethics. There is no conceivable reason why real, basic goods should ever cease to be valued. Thus, there is no reason to believe that the commands of the natural law are rescinded even in the beatific vision.

If contemplation of God were an alternative to participation in basic human goods, then one might expect divine

---

4*Summa Contra Gentiles* III, 9, [1].
5*Summa Theologiae* I-II, 18, 6.

law, which comes directly from God, to differ from natural
law, which we know through being human. But this is
not the case. Aquinas says that the divine law does not
tell us anything ethically that is not in the natural law.
God's will is not a different and better guide than the
natural law within us; it is that law brought to perfection.
Grace (God's activity) never destroys nature, but perfects
it. God does not destroy free will by creating and moving
it to action. God does not destroy human fulfillment by
being our ultimate happiness. All is gift. God does not
owe anyone anything, and therefore his gift is free and
there could be no reason for him to take it back. God does
not need us, nor does he lose anything because we have
something. To say what the beatific vision is like is
beyond the scope of this book, and beyond all natural reason. What God *can* give us, one cannot say, for one cannot comprehend the divine power and will. But if he
gives it to *us*, we must be there to receive it, and we can be
sure that it will not destroy us. God does not offer us in
this life ethical standards different from those of the natural law, nor, in the beatific vision, a nature totally unlike
our present human nature. What he offers us is love to
perfect our activity, so that we might really be what we
were created to be–human beings who do not fail to be
human.

Granted that there are basic goods, what role do they
play in our ethical lives? How do they help guide our
actions? This is an important issue because almost every
ethical philosopher, at some point or another, comes
round to showing how his system protects or fosters such
things as life, friendship, and community. Most philosophers are common-sensical enough to recognize the
importance of these goods. However, the role of such

fundamental goods within the systems varies widely. If our ethical actions are to be justified, it is important that we do not misunderstand the place and function of these goods in guiding us to the ethically good and happy life. Let us begin by setting aside those possibilities for the role of the basic goods in morality which are incompatible with the freedom and reason we know we have. Through this procedure, the clarity and correctness of Aquinas's position may show itself the more obvious.

The first general position to be set aside is the model of determinism. Our knowledge of the basic goods does not determine what we shall do. These goods do not make their demands upon us in such a way that we cannot help but respect them. This is quite obvious, since we certainly do violate these goods. But notice that if ethics is a matter of responding to pleasure and pain (as it is for emotivism, social contract theory, and utilitarianism), then we act of necessity and hence do not *choose* to violate anything at all. If one buys into a theory of ethics in which first place is given to pleasure and pain (and only second to such human goods as friendship, community, and knowledge), one must accept the brazen assertion that neither oneself, nor anyone else, does anything wrong. Although we do use such language as "Follow your feelings, and you will do the right thing," if we *really* were ruled by our feelings (pleasant and painful), we would have to follow them, and there would be no sense in asking someone to decide to do so, nor in disapproving of anyone's actions. Pleasure and pain are responses in a material being to a material environment. Matter operates according to necessary laws. So, if pleasure and pain guide us, we are determined. As determined, one will never do anything wrong (or right) because there will be no real choices being made.

All will be done by instinctual response to pleasure and pain.

I have said that emotivism, social contract theory, and utilitarianism all have pleasure and pain as first principles, but it is obvious that they differ quite a bit on what they do with these first principles. Therefore, let me take a minute to discuss the specific ways that they claim moral rules are derived, and the deficiencies in these ways. Emotivism, or the theory that one should follow one's feelings, might claim that by following one's feelings one will naturally respect the basic goods of life, knowledge, friendship, etc. David Hume argued, for example, that we are all naturally possessed of a benevolent impulse which moves us to love humanity, and this makes us ethical. The question immediately arises, do we have such an impulse? In the face of the evidence of our selfishness and greed as children and, alas, as adults, it does not seem very obvious that we are possessed of a benevolent impulse. If we are, and it is natural and a matter of inevitable causality, how is it that we do not follow it? That we do not is too obvious to need argument. If we are to choose to follow the benevolent impulse, then we have stepped outside the allowable parameters of pleasure/pain motivation, and by presupposing free choice have implicitly allowed that reason plays an essential role in our doing right. At this point we are no longer in emotivism. What is more, what it means to be benevolent is not immediately clear. Some might interpret benevolence as giving everyone as much pleasure as possible; others might think benevolence means helping people to help themselves live a life of dignity which might involve some refusal of pleasure; at the far extreme, some might think benevolence would be to kill others to prevent them from having to face the inevitable miseries that attend life.

What it *means* to follow the benevolent impulse needs to be spelled out, and this, again, is a job for reason, not emotion.

The social contract theory (also known as "egoism") states very simply that the best way for anyone to get pleasure and avoid pain is to enter into a contract with others in which one agrees to restrict one's aggressive actions, provided others will restrict theirs. A social contract theorist might very well speak of fundamental human goods which need to be safeguarded, but the reason for safeguarding them is not because they are good in themselves and for all human beings, but because the individual, looking out for number one, will benefit most in terms of his or her own egotistical desires if they are honored. In other words, the laws made under a social contract are not based on the natural law, as Aquinas describes it, but on what the majority decides best suits the individual desires of those who constitute the majority. The laws are not ultimately based on reason, but on the pleasure and pain of the individuals in the social contract. Law, in such a society, is a technique for gaining pleasure and avoiding pain. Again, if the society claims its laws conform to what is true and good for all human beings, then the theory is no longer at root social contract, but has turned to the natural law for its foundation.

In utilitarianism, what is right is what brings the greatest good to the greatest number of people. This sounds quite compatible with natural law with its foundations in a natural understanding of the basic goods. Mill, himself, spoke of a hierarchy of goods: goods of virtue and knowledge are better than goods of bodily pleasure. What could be more agreeable? The only trouble is that Mill, as you will remember, did not mean that knowledge and virtue are good in themselves, but that they are good because they bring pleasure. He just thought that mental goods bring about a "better" kind of pleasure than bodily goods. The problem with this judgment is that "better" can have only one meaning in his vocabulary and that is "more pleasurable." One is stuck with the not-very-illuminating statement that mental pleasures are better than sense pleasures simply because they are more pleasurable. The attempt to distinguish more and less valuable kinds of pleasure is doomed to failure if the only judge of value is pleasure. The directive must still be: maximize pleasure and minimize pain. The appeal is still to pleasure and pain as the ultimately exclusive motivating forces in all we do. There is not a range of basic goods for the utilitarian: the meaning of the word good is reduced ultimately to pleasure.

The founder of utilitarianism, Jeremy Bentham, wanted to do ethics by the scientific method. In order to do ethics as science, whatever is considered to be really motivating us must be able to be measured: it must be physical and external (i.e., objective). Feelings or emotions meet the first specification, but they are internal and impossible to measure objectively. Motives of reason, such as justice or mercy, fail to meet either specification and so are completely out of the picture. Only pleasure and pain, as consequences of an act, meet both of these criteria. Utilitarianism moves away from motives entirely and concentrates on results. Consequences of pleasure and pain alone are to be taken into consideration in judging an act to be good or bad. Good or evil intentions are not real. If I intend to kill an innocent person, but fail, and only wound him so that he goes to a hospital where he meets and falls in love with a nurse and lives happily ever after, then I have done a good act, for the consequences of my act brought more pleasure than pain. Conversely, if I give food to a poor man to keep him from starving, and he later kills another person, then my act was wrong, regardless of my motives.

By making pleasurable and painful consequences the criteria for evaluating our actions, the utilitarian seems to get away from the subjectivism of emotivism or egoism (social contract theory), and appears to be basing ethics on reason. But this is only an appearance. Reason, as in social contract theory, is merely a technique for getting what one wants–pleasure and freedom from pain. When we ask why one should want pleasure and pain, the answer cannot be anything other than pleasure and pain. There is no objective value of pleasure and pain; if they operate as motivating forces, they do so subjectively. Utilitarianism says that we should maximize pleasure for everyone, but there is nothing in pleasure itself that can tell us that we ought to provide pleasure for others. Pleasure is particular to this person at this time. It is fantasy to think that pleasure can somehow recommend caring for others now and in the future. If one's obligation extends beyond oneself and the moment, then it does so because of something besides pleasure and pain; it does so because of reason which, by being able to transcend space and time, recognizes the value of other people. And if other people are valuable, it is not merely as pleasure-seeking things, but as beings which can participate in the basic goods.

There is one more general way in which the basic goods might be said to operate which also needs to be considered. Compatible with all three theories just discussed is the idea that one does right and avoids doing wrong because of rewards and punishments. In emotivism, if one does wrong, one will have a bad feeling; in social contract theory, if one does wrong, one will be punished by the powers of the society; in utilitarianism, rewards and punishments would be part of the net balance of pleasure and pain to be considered in any decision. What about natural law theory? Even ethics based on absolute moral values is sometimes interpreted (Nietzsche, for example) as having force only because God has the power to punish and reward. We do what God says because we fear hell and hope for heaven. Interpreted in this way, natural law ethics turns out ultimately to be another form of utilitarianism only on a grander scale. But this interpretation is *not* correct. For one thing, religious proponents of the natural law (most notably the Roman Catholic Church) have never said that morality depends on what God has revealed to us in the Bible: moral obligation is based on the nature of the human being. For another, the requirements of absolute values have essentially nothing to do with future results of actions; the criterion for judging an act right or wrong is contained essentially in the motive, which is what is intended, the purpose of the act. If the action is the kind that is bound to have consequences which one ought to consider and yet one does not consider them, then the act is indeed wrong, but not essentially because of what happens, but because of a faulty intention, a lack of care.

We have now arrived at the core of natural law ethics: to act in a careless manner is wrong. Why? It cannot be because of the actual external results, for it is easy to think up situations in which carelessness has resulted in something good. The reason it is universally wrong is because it is acting in contradiction: one disvalues what one really cares about. Immoral acts immediately and inevitably hurt the one being careless. They are self-destructive. What one is after in activity is happiness. Happiness is not merely a life of pleasure, but the fullest participation in the basic human goods, such as life, knowledge, friendship, and aesthetic experience. Such a fulfillment depends

on reasonable activity, and carelessness is opposed to this.
Hence careless activity destroys happiness. We are constantly involved in creating who we are; every moral
action either contributes to our really being human or to
some extent destroys us. There are no indifferent choices.
As Aquinas says: "Every action of a human being which
proceeds from deliberate reason is either good or bad."[6]
The law of the land may indeed "wink" at offenses, and of
course it could not, and should not, punish every kind of
wrongdoing; nevertheless, every unreasonable, and hence
wrong, action committed does affect the one acting, making him or her less human and hence less happy.

Here the meaning of the old adage "the end does not
justify the means" becomes clear. The essential reason
why good results do not justify a bad action is because
they cannot: the damage has been done. Any bad action
is bad because of a bad intention. When I do an action
that I know to be wrong for the sake of a future "greater"
good, the good result may or may not come to be, for it
depends on other activities which I do not control. But
the damage done to me is immediate and certain. Every
wrong act makes me less human, which means I am less
happy. Of course, the bad results of bad actions add to
the gravity of the wrongdoing, because they were part of
the intention (or perhaps a result of careless inattention);
but good results do not make a bad action any better. We
damage ourselves by acting contrary to reason, that is,
contrary to what we know to be good. This damage cannot be corrected by the accidental fact of good results. If it
is to be corrected, repentance is required–literally, a turning in a new direction. The trouble is, the more we act in
one way, the harder it becomes to change our direction.

---

[6]*Summa Theologiae* I-II, 18, 9.

We are creatures of habit as well as reason, and bad habits are hard to break even when we know they should be broken.

There is a passage which brings into sharp focus this center of morality. Aquinas writes: "The man who kills himself sins more gravely than he who kills another."[7] Common contemporary morality tends to think that anything is all right so long as it does not harm another. Aquinas is flatly denying this comfortable belief. Every deliberate act, whether it affects another or not, makes the doer of the action either better or worse: there are no indifferent choices. Aquinas holds suicide to be a greater offense than murder precisely because it destroys morality root and branch. Suicide is the rejection of all value and obligation. Each one of us is a center of morality, a world of morality, possessing the first principles of ethical behavior as immediately and naturally present to reflection. One is obliged to be moral not because someone tells one to, even if that someone be God, but because one tells oneself. Morality is not *extrinsic* coercion but *intrinsic* encouragement to be happy. To take one's own life is to destroy a world of morality. It is to reject purposefully all meaning in the making of choices.

This notion which holds ethics to be essentially a matter of what happens to the doer is not new with Aquinas. Plato said the same thing, and so did Aristotle. From natural reason Plato had learned that one must never do wrong, even if one has been wronged. "Turn the other cheek" is a requirement of reason as well as religion. This is not because the one who wronged one should not be harmed; he may very well deserve it. Nevertheless, one must never do wrong because it destroys oneself. It is

---

[7]*Summa Theologiae* I-II, 73, 9 ad 2.

worse to do harm, or even will harm, than it is to be harmed. Plato even goes so far as to say that the only thing worse than doing evil is doing evil and not being punished for it. Why? Because the doer of the evil is harmed by doing it, and, if not corrected, will lead an unhappy life. Getting away with evil, avoiding punishment, far from assuring happiness, assures misery. Thus, the threat of punishment does not move the ethical person, for such a person, should he do wrong, would seek, not avoid, the punishment. Every act makes us to be one kind of person or another, and every act of unrepented evil remains with us, chaining us to our passions, preventing reason and freedom from operating in us. Such a prison is not happiness.

It may appear that this ethics is selfish even though we are intent on our "better" self. Such an impression, however, is false. Happiness based on reason is unlike "happiness" based on pleasure in that it is not confined to oneself. Understood good, which is what a value is, is universal. If we know that anything is good, then we know it to be good for all, for reason understands what is universal. It makes no sense to speak of my reason and your reason. Sure enough, I think and you think, but the content of the thought, if correct, is the same for all. Thus, the basic goods, valued by the happy (good) person, extend to all human beings. Participation in the basic goods cannot be understood as my participation for my sake alone, for what is understood is always universal. The basic goods are open-ended: they are not just for me, and our participation in them is never completely achieved.

Unlike pleasure and the material goods on which it focuses, real happiness is not a question of me first. There is no need for such an attitude, for the more others participate in the basic goods, the more I can as well. My knowledge, aesthetic appreciation, and friendship all increase when others participate in these activities. To deny others full participation in the basic goods is to deny that friendship and social life are good in and for themselves. Since friendship is certainly a basic human good, it is clear that individual good is not at odds with communal good.

When we say that the essence of ethics lies in the intention of the one who acts, we are not removing the agent from the obligation to the community, but rather removing care for the external consequences from the center of ethical obligation. In fact, by focusing on the intention of the agent, we are guaranteeing care for the community in a way that concern only for consequences can never do. Consequences are unknown and can be projected in many kinds of ways so as to allow almost any action to be justified in terms of long-range results. Basing actions on consequences opens the door to "end-justifies-means" kinds of choices in which anything at all may be done if it looks as if it might bring good consequences. When this happens, the participation of the individual members of the community in the basic goods is threatened. On the other hand, if one cares that one's actions do not violate the basic goods, this includes not violating the participation of others in the basic goods.

The following of reason because it is good for oneself is not selfishness, for reason transcends the self. It is insofar as we have reason that we have language to communicate with others as equals; it is insofar as we are reasonable that we have knowledge to share with others; and it is insofar as we are reasonable that we recognize goods which must be universally valued and never violated. What is good for the individual is simultaneously good for the community. Real individual happiness involves promoting the happiness of others as well.

To understand that ethics is a question of reason and universal goods also puts to rest the notion that ethics can be out-of-date (or up-to-date) or that ethics is a matter of where one lives. Time and place do not direct the activities of reason. If they did, then the activity would fail to be reason. That ethics could change, because times change, involves the fatal picture-thinking which replaces truth with my idea of truth, and thinking with imagination and emotion. Unless there are some basic values known by reason to be always good, then there are no obligations at all. Conversely, if there really is such a thing as obligation, if there is anything at all which we ought not to do, then there are some fundamental goods which we may not violate anytime or anywhere.

As for faith, let me just say that the image of Christianity as offering pie in the sky is simply wrong. It is true that insofar as one is a Christian and believes in life after death (we have shown that this is a reasonable belief), one is sensibly interested in what that life after death will be like. This, I suppose, can be read as an interest in rewards and punishments. And of course, like little children, we sometimes only get the point of doing something if we are promised something or threatened. But the center of Jesus' message is "Repent, for the kingdom of heaven is now." We participate in heaven *now* insofar as with the grace of God we do good; insofar as we do evil, we participate in hell *now*. Every act makes us to be a certain kind of person. What I will contrary to the basic goods (what reason tells me is good, or would tell me if I listened instead of gratifying my pleasures) diminishes me, makes me less human and happy right now. What I will in accordance with the basic goods makes me more human now. How to be human is what Jesus shows us, for Jesus is perfectly human. In addition, he offers us the divine grace, the love, to help us be human. What we know of God by natural reason–that he is creator, sustainer, and mover of all things (even free will)–does not require us to believe in his love, but it does require us to acknowledge that all we are and do depends on him. Thus, although reason does not require one to accept faith in a God who is love, it certainly does not offer any real impediments to such a faith.

We are now prepared to address that most puzzling of problems, the problem of evil. It is probably the reason most often cited by atheists for not believing in God. It is therefore imperative that it be addressed in order that the whole scope of Aquinas's thought and this book have any merit at all, for the distinctions we have been making depend on knowing God the creator to exist. The problem of evil involves the apparent incompatibility of three statements: God is good; God is all-powerful; there is evil in the world. Any two of these statements can coexist perfectly well together, but it is not at all clear how all three can. It is easy to understand how there can be evil if God is good but not all-powerful: some other being causes the evil. Or it is easily understood how there can be evil in the world if God is all-powerful and not good: God is bent on doing evil or is indifferent to good and evil. Or finally, one can understand the logic of saying that if God is perfectly good and all-powerful, then there is no evil. The trouble with these three ways of dealing with the problem is that they either do not give an accurate portrait of God (no traditional believer would allow that God is not perfectly good and all-powerful) or they falsify the world (the presence of evil is all too real).

Before seeing how Aquinas addresses the problem, let us consider each of the possible solutions mentioned above in more detail, along with Aquinas's reasons for denying them as adequate. First, consider the suggestion that God is perfectly good, but not all-powerful. This is the position known as dualism, which we met in Chapter Two. It is standard to much eastern religious thought (Hinduism in particular), was held by some ancient Greek philosophers (notably Pythagoras), and was the theory of many of the heretical gnostic sects of Christianity. According to the dualist position, there is not one all-powerful being in the world, but two equally "most" powerful beings who are locked in a constant battle. One of them is good–the principle of light, of life, and of immaterial reality; the other is evil–the principle of darkness, of destruction, and the material world. Neither is prior to nor more powerful than the other. Their co-presence as principles of the universe explains the round of light and dark, life and death, as well as the endless struggle of good and evil. This position is, of course, incompatible with there being a God who is creator–that is, a cause not just of the cycles within the universe but of the universe itself. The requirement that there be a cause for all things makes dualism impossible. Whatever be the reason for evil, it cannot be that God lacks power, for no existing thing escapes from divine power, since God is the creator of all.

Perhaps God is not perfectly good, or he is indifferent to what happens to us. The answer to this question is a bit more complicated, for we need to get a hold on the difference between good and evil. What does it mean to say that something or someone is good or bad? Consider some particular thing first. What is a good saw? It is one which does the job of sawing well. This involves a number of things: that it be made of a hard material (not, for example, Styrofoam or cheese); that it have sharp teeth; that it have a handle, etc. What makes for a bad saw is that it does not do the job of cutting well. This may happen because it lacks any one of the things we mentioned, or many more that are necessary for a saw to work well. What makes a good racehorse? It must be strong, healthy, fast, etc. If it lacks any of these things, then it is a bad racehorse. Thus we can see that goodness is a matter of a thing doing what its nature indicates it should do, and badness or evil is its failure to measure up to expectation. A bad saw is one which does not have something that a saw needs to cut well; a bad racehorse is one which lacks something it needs to run fast.

In a similar way, a good human being is one who does human things well, and an evil human being is one who fails to do what a fully actual human being would do. In terms of moral good and evil (which is the issue), a good human being follows reason, and an evil human being rejects reason. Thus, for all things, goodness is the actual fulfilling of a thing's nature, and badness is the failure to be fulfilled. Since God is the cause of all that is real and actual, he cannot be the cause of evil, for evil is not an actual thing, but a defect in a thing. Thus, one may not say that the source of all that exists and that is good (insofar as it exists) is not good.

As to the possibility of God just being indifferent, this is ruled out by what we said concerning providence. God not only keeps all things in being, but directs each thing to its action. So far from being ignorant of or indifferent to what happens in the world, he is the very source of every activity.

If we cannot say that God lacks power or goodness, can we say that evil is unreal? Many defenders of a good, all-powerful God have said so. Liebniz, after having said very much what we just said about why God cannot lack power or be the cause of evil, proceeded to affirm that this is the best of all possible worlds and that evil is always beneficial in the end. That God allows evil is excused by saying that the evil things that happen to people are always learning experiences and/or deserved, and so evil can always be seen in a good light. God must permit evil, or he could not create a being with free will. Since free will is such an important good, God is justified in creating us with free will even though this means that we might do evil.

Aquinas will not accept this way out of the problem. Evil, although not a real thing existing on its own, is nevertheless a real–all too real–feature of our world. It is not true absolutely that the world could not be better, for God can always make a better thing. And it is not true that God could not make a free being who could not sin, for God can do anything that is not a contradiction, and, although it may seem so to us who are sinners, it is not necessary for us to sin to be free. In fact our sinning is an indication of our lack of freedom, of our enslavement to the passions which are not free. Faced with evil in our world and ourselves, we must never calmly accept it as a means to good (though we may believe that God can bring good out of evil). If we are not astonished and appalled at every evil we see, then we are less than human. It may be true that evil suffered may issue in growth if suffered patiently, but evil done issues in no good whatsoever. This is because the essence of evil done is in the doer, and every act of evil that is done is pure loss to the one doing it. Doing evil is a waste of one's humanity; it is self-destruction; it is a living death.

Thus, Aquinas will deny none of the three propositions which constitute the problem of evil. First of all, God must be all-powerful since he is the cause of everything. Secondly, since everything is good to the extent that it is actual, God is the cause of all goodness and of nothing evil. Finally, there is obviously evil in the world: to deny it one must be either deranged or uncaring (itself evidence of evil in the world).

When considering evil, one can speak of two kinds–physical and moral. Aquinas does not find physical evil particularly mysterious or difficult to reconcile with God's goodness and power. God created an ordered universe full of different kinds of things in mutual relation. Some of these things are material. He could not have made a material universe in which things come to perfection in time without there being some destruction of life for other life. And when one tries to explain what is wrong in this give-and-take, one discovers that there is no explanation of natural activities which shows them to be absolutely bad. Explanation is always in terms of what is actual, and what is actual is good. The death of the lamb is the life of the lion; the sickness of the human being is the thriving of the virus. The death of the lamb and the sickness of the person are certainly bad for them, but this is a relative badness, one which is good for some other creature in the universal order of things. Every evil can be explained in terms of some good, and the good can be verified by natural reason in its operation which we call science. A positive account (one which gives a reason or explanation for some interaction) is a verification of the goodness of creation.

Beyond being reconcilable with the existence of God, Aquinas says that the presence of this kind of evil in the world actually proves that God exists: "If there is evil, God exists."[8] It is only because there is order among things that there is physical evil, and this order among all things is the greatest good of the created universe, greater than any particular creature. For in the causality exemplified by the interaction of things, the activity of God is better reflected than in any one thing, for we know God as cause. A universe in which there was no interaction among things would be a less perfect universe.

The real bafflement and mystery comes in with the consideration of moral evil. There is no balance here; there is no gain which can explain the need for the loss. There is no positive explanation available in terms of good, at least not one accessible to natural reason. Essentially, moral evil is dead loss; it does nothing but destroy.

How then can a good, all-powerful God allow for such a thing? It is true that he is not directly the source of evil, for he is the cause of all that has being, and evil is a defect in being reasonable. But is he not the indirect cause since he is the cause of all activity, including every act of free choice? Although he is not the cause of the badness of a choice, it seems that he could, if he willed, withhold his cooperation and the evil deed would not be done. Why, then, if he is good, does he not do this? Is he not guilty of neglect here, and thus ultimately accountable for the evil in the world? After all, he made the world and does not prevent evil from occurring, which he could do.

I think, however, that such a charge of negligence will not stick. For anyone to be guilty of neglect, there must be something that he ought to be doing but fails to do. But there is nothing that God ought to be doing. He is not so related to his creation as to owe it anything. It makes no sense to say that he owes human beings anything, that he

---

[8]*Summa Contra Gentiles* III, 71, [10].

should prevent them from sinning. If he does, we are the better for it: this is grace. If he does not, he cannot be said to be unfair, for it is not his job to keep us from sinning. He has given us reason which, if we follow it, will keep us from sinning. If we do not follow it, it can in no way be said to be his fault. The creator of all things is not under obligation to his creation. Why God permits sin, we cannot say, for we cannot know the divine plan and will. But we can say that his allowing it is not a breech of contract, nor an injustice to his creation.

Does what we have said explain why there is moral evil? Unfortunately, no. Moral evil remains a profound mystery. It really cannot be explained. Why would one do what one knows one does not really want to do? Why would one place a stumbling stone in the way of happiness? There is no reason for this; it is wholly unreasonable. Although sin remains an ultimate mystery, it is not at all remote or unknown to us. While it is not metaphysically real, but a lack of real being (of being reasonable), it is all too real in the sense that it makes all the difference in our happiness. One need only look out on our world of hatred, violence, and injustice to know the kind of reality that evil has. Or worse, one may look into one's own heart and recognize with bafflement and grief, the real, crippling presence of evil.

But let me repeat that the presence of evil in our world in no way proves that God does not exist or that, if he exists, he must be either evil or lack power. Our basis for saying that God exists lies in the fact that the universe of things cannot explain its existence, and so we say there is a creator of all things. Such a creator is the cause of everything that has real being. The activities of all things are real and are traceable back to the creator. Therefore, God has power over all things, including human free will. God is the cause of what is real in our free choices, but since evil has no real being of its own (it is a defect in the good of being reasonable), God is not the direct cause of evil. And, although God could prevent moral evil by refusing to cooperate in our bad choices, he is under no obligation to do so.

In this chapter, we have looked at the meaning of human happiness and found it to lie in the doing and promoting of the basic human goods. To violate these goods is to violate ourselves and our happiness. God as creator is the source of our being and our reason, and hence of all the basic human goods. One can say, therefore, that in God lies our happiness. But when we say this, we must be careful to remember the great difference knowing God as creator makes to this statement. Plato and Aristotle considered the ultimate happiness of contemplating God to be an alternative to participating in human goods basically because they thought of God as one thing among many, as the highest part of an eternal universe. For this reason there is really no such thing as *human* happiness for Plato and Aristotle. Happiness is divinity. To be happy is to be divine and thus to cease to be human. Thomas Aquinas understood that God is not a part of the universe and therefore that he can never be an alternative to nature, not even in the beatific vision. While Plato and Aristotle speak of the divinization of the human being as being happiness, for Aquinas it is really a matter of the humanization of the human being. Indeed, Aquinas can speak in both ways, for he understood God to be the creator and perfector of nature and hence never a replacement. To be graced by God is not incompatible with being human: it is to be more surely and purely human. Human happiness lies in being fully human, perfectly human. For Aquinas, unlike his Greek predecessors, there really is such a thing as *human* happiness, that is, *human* perfection.

The great hurdle to being fully human is moral evil. We are responsible for this, not God. Although we could not use our free will at all without God, he is not the cause of our evil choices. God is the cause of all that is real in our actions, but evil is a falling away from the real exercise of reason, and thus God does not cause evil. God gives us reason, but we refuse to use it. Why? There is no reason; no justification can be given.

Reason's consideration of human happiness and our failure to achieve it has brought us once again to the edge of wonder. First of all, we have found that the apparent antagonism between the position which claims that human happiness lies in God and the position which claims that it cannot lie in God and be human proves to be wonderfully dissolved by clarifying what we mean by God and human happiness. Reason tells us that God is creator, which means two things. One, he has freely made creatures of particular natures; and two, his activity in his creation does not eradicate those created natures. Thus, God does not fulfill human beings by replacing them. Reason also tells us that human happiness is not merely the material state of pleasure and absence of pain. It is to be found in pursuing and participating in basic human goods recognized by reason to be inexhaustibly rich. The open-endedness of these goods indicates that they do not confine us to imperfection. Human perfection or happiness turns out to be, not the replacement of properly human kinds of activity by some other "higher" kind of activity which we call divinity, but the perfection of properly human activity, which then is understood as what it means for a human creature to be in the presence of the creator.

Our failure to be reasonable and good, the failure that is sin, leaves us with another mystery to be pondered. Why has God allowed us to sin? And has he abandoned us to sin? Here is the edge of reason and faith to which the exercise of reason has been seen consistently to bring us. We do not know why God allows us to sin. It is not that he must, nor is it reasonable for us to think that our sinning will turn out to be the source of a greater good. As for our being abandoned to our sinning, reason may be some help here. Since God is the source of every good, we know that whatever good we do is done in cooperation with God. And since evil is a defect in the good of reason, every evil action is, in a way, the refusal to cooperate with God's activity. It is our reasonable acts which accept God's help, and our unreasonable acts which reject it. Help is offered us. Of this we can be sure, for we know that all our good choices are only done with God's cooperation. We may or may not accept the offer. Natural reason cannot explain the how and why of grace, but it can tell us that since God is not an alternative to reason but its source and support, it can never be reasonable to refuse grace. Thus, the act of faith cannot be considered an unreasonable act, but, on the contrary, appears to be rather more reasonable than its alternative.

VI
Reason and Love

Thomas Aquinas presents the world with revolutionary answers to the two great questions of philosophy. To the question "Why?" he answers with the radical notion of God as creator. To the question "Who am I?" he answers with the uncompromised vision of the unity of the human being.

The world raises a question for us that the world cannot answer: "Why is there a world at all?" This is a non-scientific question in the sense that it cannot be verified by the scientific method, for there is no possibility of measuring or detecting through experiment the cause of all being. But in another sense, it is *the* ultimate scientific question, for it is the taking of the question "Why?" all the way to the root of reality. The literal meaning of science, the meaning it bore up until the Renaissance and the birth of modern science, is simply "knowledge." Science in this sense is about knowledge of what is real, and surely the source of all reality must be considered real and worthy of thought and wonder. It certainly is for the pagan philosophers Plato and Aristotle. Their philosophies, although obviously not based on Revelation, culminate in a discussion of the divine. What is revolutionary about Aquinas's position is that it does not hold the divine to be the highest and most powerful of all beings within a common context, in which case, it might be in competition with them. On the contrary, the God of Aquinas is outside the context of things: he is the creator of the context—the maker and sustainer of the universe.

Oddly enough, the more radical notion of God as creator, which held God to be a cause unlike other causes discovered by science, guarantees the validity of the scientific quest to understand the world in a way that the pagan idea of God could not do. As creating cause, God makes it false to say that his causality is the only real causality: the created things of the universe, with all their causal relationships, really do exist. Therefore, God's causality is not the only explanation for the way the world is. God the creator is not an alternative to natural explanation: he is the explanation for that explanation. He explains the existence of natural knowledge of the world by explaining the existence of the world.

As for Aquinas's radical notion of human being, this guarantees the validity of the range of human pursuits from knowledge to free choices to the quest for human happiness. The human being is a thinking animal, the unity of immaterial and material being. The *only* way science can be justified is by admitting that we have an activity (thinking) which transcends the material world that science studies. Universal statements about the structure of reality could never issue from the particularity of material things, since material things are always isolated from each other by the nature of time and space—while Rover and Spot are both dogs, they are not the same

matter. The *only* way freedom and ethical obligation can
be warranted is if we transcend our material environment.
If we are merely material beings subject to determined
laws of matter, then we cannot think, we are not free, we
cannot do right or wrong, and we cannot love. Of course,
even more basically, if we are merely material beings, we
have no reason to suppose that all runs in accordance to
universal laws of matter, or even, in fact, to suppose that
we are merely material beings; for both these statements
presuppose an ability to think in universal terms, to
understand beyond the here and now.

On the other hand, the only way it makes sense for us to
be in this body and in this material world is if it is natural
for us to be so embodied. If we are really just rational
souls, then the only explanation for our being in the world
is that this is some great mistake, that the material world is
evil and we are somehow entrapped. But this makes a
mockery of our all recognition of goods, for all our basic
values presuppose a valuing of being embodied. We
value life, and life is organically transmitted from another
body; we value knowledge, and we draw our knowledge
initially from the material world through our senses; we
value beauty, and beauty is appreciated through the
senses as well as the intellect; we value friendship, and
friendship depends on communication which depends on
bodies.

This recognition that we are beings who communicate
meaningfully is crucial to understanding our nature, for
communication requires both aspects of our being: our
rationality and our materiality. We can share meaning
because meaning is something that can be shared–an
immaterial reality which can be in two places at the same
time and in the same way. And we can share meaning in
the ways we do–language, art, music–because we have the

ability, through being embodied, to make signs and to see
and hear them.

Finally, this unity really belongs to each unique individual. Knowing God as creator, Aquinas knows how it can
be that thinking beings, which can never be corrupted,
can come to be at a particular moment of time. He need
not say, with Plato, that each individual has been eternally
moving from body to body, or, with Aristotle, that each
individual borrows reason from some transcendent mind.
He can say what coincides much better with common
sense, that each individual does his or her own sensing
and thinking and began to sense and think at a certain
point in time. The rational soul cannot, indeed, be gener-
ated from the matter of the parents; it must be created.
But since creation is not something that happened once
long ago, but the constant dependence of all things on
God, there is no reason why new things may not be
created.

These two revolutionary ideas transform other problems
as well. Without the notion of God as creator, God's
providence must preclude free will; for if God is a nature
of a particular kind which is just more powerful than others and hence can dominate them, then when God acts in
another being, that being's own activity is suspended.
God the creator, however, makes the activities of all
things. His activity in a thing does not suspend that
thing's own proper activity but guarantees that the proper
activity operate. Hence, God's presence to me is my freedom. As for Aquinas's notion of the human being, obviously, if we are not rational beings but mere animals, then
we have no freedom whatever one's idea of God may be.
And if our rationality is not really our own, then again we
do not have any real freedom. Only if I can think and
hence deliberate, and only if my deliberation is really my

own–really belongs to *this* thinking animal–can I be said to have freedom. Thus, Aquinas's resolution of the problem of providence and free choice depends on his understanding of God as creator and the human being as an individual unity of rationality and animality.

When we turn to the issue of human obligation, we find these two revolutionary ideas of Aquinas again clearing the way to new insights. Only if we are thinking beings and hence free to choose, can we be obligated in any way. All that is required in the way of our being immaterial for thought and freedom is, of course, required for us to be valuers. When the questions arise as to whether ethics is purely a matter of divine fiat and whether the ultimate fulfillment of the human being is human or divine, the importance of Aquinas's teachings on God as creator and on the human being as individual embodied rationality again becomes evident. Since God the creator makes and directs all things, one might indeed say that ethics is what God decides. But what could the fiat of a creating God be like for a human being? It must be: be what you are, be human. God makes us to be human in order that we be human, that we fulfill human nature. His requirements for us are what are naturally good for us. Thus, God does not impose ethics from without, but gives us ethics by giving us existence as human beings.

Is it when we ask about the final fulfillment of the human being, that we finally make the jump between the human and the divine? No, again; for human fulfillment is not the replacement of human nature with divinity, but the perfection of human nature in divinity, that is, in love. The beatific vision is not divinization on the model of Plato or Aristotle in which human nature is forsaken in favor of divinity. Our ultimate happiness on Aquinas's model is *human* happiness, not absorption into God. In

addition, Aquinas's insistence on the permanent embodiment of the human being corroborates this point. A properly human activity is one which involves the whole
human being, body and soul.

Our pursuit of the basic human goods is the pursuit of
embodied reason, for, as we detailed above, all these values have something to do with being embodied. Aquinas's insistence on the resurrection of the body as our final
state is meaningless if our happiness is to be a disembodied contemplation and absorption into God. Human
happiness is just that–the fulfillment of all that it is to be
human.

It is Thomas Aquinas's great devotion to reason that
allows him to so deepen the philosophical explanations of
God and human being. Some might rise up at this point
and say, with the Protestant reformers, that this devotion
to reason is Aquinas's very problem, that he lets reason get
in the way of faith. Others might object from the other
side, in the name of science and philosophy, that Aquinas's religious commitment ruins his reason. It should,
however, be clear at this point that a devotion to reason is
not in any way incompatible with a religious devotion to
God. Nor is devotion to God incompatible with devotion
to reason. To say that Aquinas is completely devoted to
reason does not make him a rationalist in the sense of one
who rejects all that does not fit in a deductive system. The
great truths which we have discussed in this book are all
matters of reaching up to open-ended, living truths which
surpass the comprehension characteristic of a closed
deductive system. Nor does saying that Aquinas is a
Christian believer vitiate the claim that he is more reasonable than his illustrious pagan predecessors Plato and Aristotle. Faith in God is faith in love, is a commitment to the
way things are (or, in the case of human nature, the way

things ought to be). God makes things be what they are, and the only possible motivation for such a gift is love. We saw that God as creator is the guarantor of science, not its demise. He is the guarantor that what we know of human nature is really true of human nature. He is the guarantor that human beings are really free, and that there really is such a thing as human responsibility and happiness.

As making things to be is the act of love on God's part, so knowing how things are requires an act of love on our part. Aquinas understands knowing not on the model of snapshots of reality–static images of one-to-one correspondence of what is real with a picture in the mind–but as a dynamic activity of formulating and reformulating the truth as new elements of the mystery that is reality raise new questions. He says, in one place, that we do not fully know the essence of even the simplest thing. Knowing is a complex, multi-level affair. It involves the reception of sense data by which we are in continuity with a material world, the formulation of ideas which explain that world, and the judgment as to whether the ideas do correctly express the way the world is. New sense data and new ideas raise new questions for judgment. Did I understand correctly? How can I account for this previously unrecognized bit of information? This procedure advances toward a more complete understanding of the way things are only under the directive of a moral concern. Unless we value knowledge, we shall never attain it. We are not passive receptors recording automatically like video cameras the way the world is. We are questioning animals, and questioning is not an automatic process. We must decide whether we will hear the question. We can easily shut off the questioning because of impatience, weariness, fear, or prejudice. We can easily kill the life that is

knowing. Presupposed to finding the truth is the unwav-
ering commitment to the good of knowledge: this is a
moral act without which philosophy, which is the life of
natural reason, cannot be.

We said at the end of Chapter Four that considering
human freedom is the closest we come to seeing God's
activity. The operation of freedom in morality presents us
with another way of talking about God and, ultimately,
about human happiness. Every act that is freely chosen
makes something new, both in the sense that each free act
is a brand new thing unexplainable by the workings of the
rest of the universe, and in the sense that each freely chosen act shapes the character of the agent. By one's
choices, one creates ethical character. If one asks what is
the motivation to create what we would recognize as good
actions, we catch a glimpse of what could motivate God to
create.

The name we give to this purest of motivations is, of
course, love. This is not to get sentimental or theological,
but to attempt to specify what is behind both the human
creative activity of making good choices and the divine
activity of creating all things. The reason why God creates
cannot be any kind of coercion, for God is first cause; nor
could it be any kind of obligation, for nothing is prior to
God's choice to create which could oblige him; nor could it
be any kind of need, whether physical or emotional or
intellectual, for God in his perfection lacks nothing. The
only candidate left seems to be what we mean by love.
When one considers the human making which is morality
at its best, the motivation for the truly moral human being
is not coercion, nor external obligation, nor need, but the
overflow of human life (one of reason and freedom) which
we call love. Of course, probably no human action is
completely free from these other kinds of motivations, but

in the purest acts of free choice we have an insight into an activity that is less unlike the divine activity than any other which we meet in our experience of the world.

It is not surprising that the meaning of the word "love" is mysterious even as we use it concerning human actions. Love is something we do not understand perfectly; yet it is not without meaning, for we know some kinds of things that it certainly is not. It is not lying, or cheating, or kill-ing. Its meaning is something we grow into, never pos-sessed completely, but recognized as the most important aspect of the reality which beckons us ever deeper into the fullness of what it is to be human. Our relation to love is quite like our relation to God the creator. And though the truth "God is Love" is given to us by the grace of Revela-tion, it is also the ultimate intelligibility of what "God" means philosophically.

In Chapter Five, we said that the presence of God to human activity is not an addition to the requirements of natural law. To believe in God does not change one's ethics nor thus one's moral commitment to the truth. This becomes clearer when we think of God's presence as the presence of love. We recognized, in the same chapter, that sin is the great unexplainable gap or defect in reality. One only does wrong if one knows an act is wrong yet nevertheless commits it. There is no ignorance that needs correcting here, no additional law to be added to the natu-ral law. We know that many of the things that we do are wrong; yet we do them. Before this mystery of sin we indeed appear helpless. What God offers us (does not require of us) is love to free us from the fears and preju-dices which keep us in self-imposed ignorance. Love, of course, cannot be a requirement, since love is a letting be–the freeing of someone to be him or herself. Thus, the presence of a religious commitment to the creating God of love is not the addition of an alternative to reason, but the underlining of reason's own requirement: the moral commitment to knowledge, which perfects the judgment, which perfects the insight, which grasps reality. The fully perfected human being, the happy human being, is the human being in love–that is, in God.

So we come to see philosophy or natural reason as it traditionally was understood–as the "love of wisdom." Love is not destroyed by reason, nor reason by love. Reason brings us to the notion of God the creator as the source of all that is real and good. When we try to understand what could motivate God to create, the only meaningful (though mysterious) explanation is love. God owes the world nothing, and is in no way perfected by the existence of the world. His creation is a perfect gift, an act of complete generosity, giving where there is no merit, and giving with no strings attached. By analyzing the human activity of thinking, which we use to attain the notion of God the creator who is love, we recognize that this activity is fruitful only if the thinker is in love with truth. Only love will let the world be even at the cost of suffering the humiliation of finding that what we thought was true is not really true, that we must break the old molds and forge ever-new ones as we reach into a world of meaning that is far deeper than we thought.

Reason operates through love as the great champion of love. Its whole life is devoted to love of truth. Its journey is strewn with the carcasses of divine dragons and inhuman beings, ideas of God and ideas of humanity which turn out to be false and threatening, and hence must be slain. It is false to think of God as the greatest and most powerful force in the universe, for he is the cause of the universe. God is not the alternative to the pursuits of natural reason, but, surprisingly and wonderfully, their great support and inspiration. It is false to think of human beings as mechanical structures of matter bound in meaningless surrender to extinction, or as souls destined to endless meaningless incarcerations in flesh. We are rational animals, material beings who nevertheless share meaning in symbol and language, and hence transcend our materiality. We are mysterious unities of the material and the immaterial, the crossroads of the many orders in creation, each one of us a permanent part of the universe and a microcosm, through what we are and can know, of that universe. It is false to think of God's providence as the negation of human freedom. He is freedom's very affirmation: without a doubt, if God is all-provident, we must be free. Nor is human freedom the great exception to God's power and knowledge: without a doubt, every act of freedom is more caused by God than by me, yet is wholly my free act. God's presence to my activity is not a part of it, but its very source–in this case, the source of life and freedom. Finally, it is false to think of God as the arbitrary dictator of ethical obligation. We need look no further than our own nature as rational animals to find the values and directives which require us to act in some ways but not others. The only way we offend God is by hurting ourselves, those very selves that God has created reasonable and free. Nor does human nature dissolve, in the end, into divinity. Human nature is real precisely because God made it so, and human happiness (the perfection of human nature) likewise is real.

Our final end and happiness, the fulfillment of all that we can be, is not to become God, but to become human. We are not human now, but deficient shadows of human beings. To do wrong is to fail to be human. Our final perfection is indeed to share in divinity: it is to share in love. Our perfection is to be loving human beings.

Far from being the cold, relentless jailer of human joy, reducing reality to pat formulations and dead deductions, reason is the gallant and loyal knight who challenges and slays the enemies of joy. It is reason who defeats ignorance, uncovers the traitor prejudice, and routs fear. Without reason, the imagination and the emotions, those treasures of our bodily life, are powerless to free the joy that gives them life. The romanticism which rejects reason rejects its life, for emotion and imagination die the death of despair in the face of the change and decay which is the inevitable lot of the animal on which they depend.

The real romance is the romance of reason. Only by attending to what can be known to be true, only by transcending emotion and imagination can we succeed in clearing the way for emotion and imagination to dance with the joy that is their life. Alone the emotions or imagination can only succeed in presenting a particular picture of reality, for emotions and imagination, as acts bound to a material body, are always about particular things. In fact, if reality could be known in a picture, then there would be no further use for the imagination and the emotions. Such a model, which sees knowing as an automatic process, has no need to seek to understand and therefore to attempt to imagine a better metaphor or analogy, nor to support the quest with fervor. And, of course, any one picture cannot possibly be true, especially when it tries to portray the ultimate source of reality or ultimate values. Since we know God to exist as the cause of all things, he is not one particular kind of thing. Any picture of God we might have must be false.

Likewise, any picture or feeling of what constitutes human fulfillment must be false. For the pursuit of the basic goods, in which lies our happiness, is an open-ended affair, never fully realized by any one person, nor by all.

Reason tells us this. Any image of human good as lying in some particular thing puts an unwarranted end to the pursuit–through an examination of conscience with the support of imagination and emotion–of the fully human life.

If we will only think, and not just imagine or feel, we shall discover that reality is more mysterious, more real, and more wonderful than we or anyone had thought or could ever imagine. Here is an open playground for the imagination and emotions. Such notions of God and human happiness as Aquinas presents to us invite reason and her aids–the imagination and emotions–to further exploration, to continued life. Since God is creator, the world and human beings, and all within them, are really real. All other notions of God, although more accessible to the imagination and flattering to the emotions, drain the world of meaning and reality. The act of creation cannot be imagined, nor can we imagine the material/immaterial unity which is the human being: these are the conclusions of reason. But the conclusions of reason are not the end of the story, but its ever-new beginning. Reason leads to mystery, to a wonder that is as profound as all existence, a wonder only discoverable by reason but reveled in without end by imagination and emotion. Under the banner of love, reason frees joy from the bonds of fear and despair and defends an everlasting and infinitely delightful home for all things human. This is the romance of reason.